ISMAIL MERCHANT'S PARIS
Filming and Feasting in France

ISMAIL MERCHANT'S
PARIS

Filming and Feasting in France

Including 40 Recipes

By Ismail Merchant

Photographs by Erica Lennard, Marina Faust, and Seth Rubin

HARRY N. ABRAMS, INC., PUBLISHERS

For Anna

Editor: Ellen Nidy
Designer: Dana Sloan

Library of Congress Cataloging-in-Publication Data
Merchant, Ismail.
    Ismail Merchant's Paris : filming and feasting in France / by Ismail Merchant.
        p.   cm.
    ISBN 0-8109-4162-7
    1. Merchant, Ismail–Anecdotes.   2. Cookery.   I. Title.
PN1998.3.M466A3   1999
791.43′0233′092–dc21   99–11027

Printed and bound in Japan

HARRY N. ABRAMS, INC.
100 FIFTH AVENUE
NEW YORK, N.Y. 10011
www.abramsbooks.com

PHOTOGRAPH CREDITS

Numbers refer to pages. Merchant Ivory Productions is abbreviated MIP.
2. Seth Rubin © MIP/Warner Bros.; 4–5. Seth Rubin © MIP; 6. James Ivory; 9. Marina Faust © MIP; 10–11. Marina Faust © MIP; 13. James Ivory; 15. Seth Rubin © MIP; 16–17. Seth Rubin © MIP; 18. Erica Lennard; 20. Erica Lennard; 21. Erica Lennard; 23. Clark Worswick © MIP/Angelika Films; 28. © MIP/Angelika Films; 29. © MIP/Angelika Films; 32–33. Erica Lennard; 37. Seth Rubin; 38–39. Seth Rubin; 40. (center, bottom) James Ivory. (top) Seth Rubin; 43. Juan Quirno © MIP/Lyric Films International; 46. Erica Lennard; 47. Erica Lennard; 48. Erica Lennard; 49. Erica Lennard; 50. Juan Quirno © MIP/Lyric Films International; 53. (top) James Ivory. (bottom) Seth Rubin; 54. Seth Rubin; 57. Juan Quirno © MIP/Lyric Films International; 58–59. Juan Quirno © MIP/Lyric Films International; 62. Seth Rubin © MIP/Warner Bros.; 64. Alain Nogues/SYGMA; 66. Alain Nogues/SYGMA; 67. Mikki Ansin © MIP/Cineplex Odeon; 69. Mikki Ansin; 71. James Ivory; 77. Seth Rubin © MIP; 78–79. Seth Rubin © MIP; 79. Seth Rubin © MIP; 80. Seth Rubin © MIP; 81. (bottom) Seth Rubin © MIP. (top) Anna Kythreotis; 83. Arnaud Borrel; 84. Seth Rubin © MIP; 85. Seth Rubin © MIP; 86–87. Erica Lennard; 89. Seth Rubin; 91. Erica Lennard; 96. Seth Rubin; 98. Erica Lennard; 99. Marina Faust; 100. Marina Faust; 101. Marina Faust © MIP; 102. Erica Lennard; 103. Erica Lennard; 104. (bottom) Marina Faust © MIP. (top) Marina Faust; 105. Marina Faust © MIP; 108. Seth Rubin © MIP; 109. Seth Rubin © MIP; 111. Marina Faust © MIP; 112. (top) Seth Rubin. (bottom) James Ivory; 115. Seth Rubin © MIP; 116. Seth Rubin; 117. Seth Rubin © MIP; 118. Seth Rubin © MIP; 120. James Ivory.

Page 2: Unchanged since the early 1900s, the Brasserie Lipp is still *the* brasserie of Paris, serving delicious food and attracting a delicious crowd of bejeweled courtesans, film and stage stars, and players from the sports and high-finance worlds, as well as intellectuals and artists from the nearby Saint-Germain-des-Prés neighborhood. This photograph was taken not in the 1940s, but during the shooting of *Surviving Picasso* in 1995.

Pages 4-5: A scene from *Jefferson in Paris* re-creating the ascent of the Montgolfier balloon at Versailles on September 19, 1783.

CONTENTS

F IRST THERE WAS the long boat journey from Bombay to Genoa. Then there was the train journey from Genoa to Paris, which, given the typically Italian conditions of overcrowding, noise, chaos, and grand-scale disorganization, was exactly like train journeys in India. And then there was my arrival in Paris.

Paris was not my ultimate destination on that first journey from India in August of 1958; that was America, where I was about to begin my studies at New York University. However, Paris had long exerted a fascination over me. I had seen many photographs of this handsome historic city; I had heard the elegant tones of its language from the songs of Maurice Chevalier on All India Radio; and I had seen French films that occasionally played at the Liberty Cinema in Bombay during the Sunday morning shows. I had seen Michel Clouzot's *Wages of Fear* with Yves Montand and also Jean Renoir's film *Rules of the Game* at the Alliance Française. I knew from books that the world's greatest artists, writers, and philosophers had been drawn to live in this sophisticated metropolis. And I had determined that some day I would go to Paris, study at the Sorbonne, and learn the French language. So, as the Genoa train pulled into the Gare de Lyon I felt a tremendous thrill—even though on this occasion I would be in Paris only long enough to get from the Gare de Lyon to the Gare du Nord in order to continue my journey to America.

In Genoa, as in India, there had been no shortage of porters at the station to help travelers with their luggage. But Parisian porters seemed scarce and I had a great deal of luggage. In addition to clothes, books, and farewell gifts, I had a large wicker hamper full of my mother's homemade pickles. Every Indian family produces its own characteristic pickle, and my mother believed that a meal without different varieties of her *aachar* was incomplete—not a meal at all. So she had made absolutely sure that for the duration of my studies in the United States I would not want for her pickles.

When I finally found a porter, he demanded his tip in advance and in dollars. I *had* dollars, but each one was already allocated to cover travel, accommodation, tuition, food, and so on. My budget was extremely tight, and to start giving dollars away to porters would have unbalanced my carefully calculated

The glass pyramids built by I. M. Pei in the forecourt of the Louvre: the newest , boldest—and by now much-loved—Parisian landmark encountered by Ismail Merchant on his way to and from his office on rue Montmarte.

finances. However, I also couldn't afford to lose what seemed to be the only porter at the Gare de Lyon.

I was aware from all I had heard and read that the French enjoy the most distinguished cuisine in the world, and this gave me a brainstorm. The practice of bartering was common in Bombay and, from what I had observed, in Genoa too. Painful though the sacrifice was, I opened my wicker hamper and offered the porter, in lieu of dollars, a jar of my mother's *aachar*, explaining to him in broken French that it was a special condiment prepared by my mother in India. However, clearly the bartering system did not operate in the French capital because the porter continued to insist on dollars, unable to see the value of my mother's specially prepared pickles.

I had no choice; there was a connecting train to catch. I gave the porter my dollars—three, I think—fewer than he demanded, but more than I could spare. To make up the shortfall I insisted he keep a jar of *aachar*. I was certain that once he had tasted this great specialty he would regret not accepting his entire tip in pickles.

So the porter and I made it to the Gare du Nord with my suitcases and packages and pickles. But I felt a sense of disappointment about the French.

⤞⤝

My next encounter with French culture and people came, paradoxically, not in France but in New York, where my first experience of French cuisine was on Manhattan's West Side. The Brittany on Ninth Avenue was an inexpensive hangout for French sailors on shore leave, French expatriates, and anyone else of meager means who liked tasty affordable French food. This simple bistro was a culinary oasis in the desert of cheap, filling junk food that was the staple diet of cash-strapped students in late 1950s New York. As I worked my way through the menu from coq au vin to beef bourguignon to pot-au-feu, I realized that the reputation of the French as masters of the kitchen was in no way exaggerated. If this were the standard of an inexpensive bistro, I could only wonder what kind of dishes were being prepared in the kitchens of the exclusive and grand French restaurants off Fifth Avenue such as Le Pavillon and La Côte Basque, whose long white window curtains discreetly veiled the wealthy diners and numerous formally dressed staff. It would be several years before I learned about, or went

Ismail Merchant at the age of twenty-two, on the eve of his departure for the United States in 1958. The mustache disappeared upon arrival in New York because, he recalls, he wanted a "new look."

8

to any, of the three-star Parisian restaurants that served as models for these restaurants in New York.

It was in New York that I saw the early films of the New Wave—by directors such as Louis Malle, Claude Chabrol, Francois Truffaut, Jean-Luc Godard—and the inspired work of Jean Renoir including *The River*, which he had shot in India. I also finally saw Marcel Carné's *Les Enfants du Paradis*.

I came to know and admire the French through their food and their films—two of the defining elements of modern French culture, both of which resonate with my own passions for cooking and filmmaking and which would, in time, lead to my happy filming and feasting in France.

Merchant and Jeanne Moreau in front of the Louvre during the filming of *The Proprietor*.

By the time I graduated from New York University I had made my first film, a short dance piece called *The Creation of Woman*, based on an Indian legend. It was nominated for an Academy Award in 1961 and accepted in competition at the Cannes Film Festival later that year.

These days the focus at Cannes is less on the substance of the films than on their commercial potential. But in 1961, despite the element of glitter and gossip, which has always been a part of this festival and part of its popularity, Cannes was taken very seriously both by filmmakers and by knowledgeable, experienced critics who were passionate about film and who were responding positively to European artistic trends in filmmaking. The great Asian directors such as Akira Kurosawa and Satyajit Ray were being honored there; the important European directors, such as Ingmar Bergman, Luis Buñuel, Federico Fellini, and Michelangelo Antonioni, were at their peak; and the films of the French New Wave were finding an audience beyond France. These sophisticated films generated a great deal of interest, and American distributors were aware that subtitled films could have respectable runs in the United States.

The thrill of being invited to Cannes was immense, and I was keenly anticipating the pleasure of seeing my film on the screen and having it evaluated by all the important pundits of the cinema—maybe even selling it. But I arrived in Cannes on the appointed day to find that the festival had rescheduled the screening—my film had been shown the previous night, and I had missed it. The administrators shrugged off the matter as if it were of no consequence. I was disappointed and furious—if I had been told I could have changed my flight from New York. But I had not been told.

I knew only one person at the festival: Gene Moskovitch, the chief film critic of *Variety*. I called him and he commiserated, even managing to lighten my bleak mood a little by telling me that he had seen my film, liked it, and had given it a very favorable review in his paper.

To make matters worse, my accreditation had not been organized, so I had

---

Merchant and Ivory take over the Place de la Concorde to film scenes for *Surviving Picasso* and *The Proprietor* set during the Nazi Occupation of Paris.

no pass for the screenings. I had nothing to do, in short, but wander along the Croisette, the main strip in Cannes that runs along the beach and is lined with hotels and restaurants. I had two days in Cannes before I was to leave for India where I was planning to make my first feature film with James Ivory—it was the start of our collaboration. I had heard that Cannes would be swarming with investors and important film financiers during the festival, so I thought I might still turn this fiasco to my advantage by finding these angels who would give me money to make my film. But the investors eluded me and I had to begin my journey to India, and my journey into independent filmmaking, without their money.

Although technically I was a participant in the festival, in reality I was merely an observer. So I watched the show: the stars all dressed up (or undressed), and the important, busy people dashing around on urgent business. Everyone, it seemed, had somewhere to be, something vital to do.

The festival had arranged accommodation for me at the Carlton Hotel, the grandest in Cannes, where all the movie stars and important people stay. So, I was in the embarrassing situation of living at one of the most expensive hotels in the world with scarcely two cents to my name. Eating at the Carlton restaurant or ordering room service was out of the question. Eating at any of the smart places along the Croisette was also impossible. I scrutinized the menus outside the modest bistros lining the narrow side streets to see if I could afford even the cheapest meal.

It was in these bistros where I discovered that the French prepare inexpensive ingredients with the same care and imagination that they use for creating the most expensive dishes. An omelet, for example, came out not as the lumpy, tasteless dish often encountered elsewhere, but as a light, fluffy cloud. An omelet *aux fines herbs*, with its subtle hint of fresh parsley and chives, transformed beaten eggs into a feast. Even a salad, dressed with a sharp vinaigrette and accompanied by some cheese, and chunks of a crusty baguette—the best bread in the world—was in a class of its own. I am very fond of fish and once, with an appetite sharpened by all the walking I was doing and, perhaps, by the sparkling waters of the Mediterranean, I ordered the cheapest fish on the menu. This was my introduction to *rouget*—red mullet. The firm, sweet-flavored flesh of the *rouget* was perfectly balanced by its simple coating of olive oil and lemon juice, and it has since become one of my favorite dishes in France.

On my last evening I went over to the old Palais, the very heart of the festival, to see the stars and producers and directors arrive for that night's screening, and to watch them ascend the wide red-carpeted staircase. However, I could see nothing but the backs of heads and the explosions of a thousand flashbulbs—the crowd was impenetrable, the noise of the yelling photographers and cheering spectators deafening. I walked away, wondering if a time would ever come when I would walk up the red-carpeted staircase and the photographers' lenses would be turned on me.

→>-<←

In 1965 we submitted our second film, *Shakespeare Wallah*, to the Berlin Film Festival—an event that would indirectly solidify our relationship with France. Jim and I flew to Berlin to await the verdict on whether the film would be selected for competition, but with the decision still several days away we decided to take the train to Paris.

So, six years after the pickle incident I returned to Paris. This time I arrived bearing not pickles, but an acutely painful ear infection that made me feel very low. Jim took me to an outdoor concert opposite Notre Dame, and after the concert we crossed the bridge that links the Ile de la Cité with the neighboring Ile

The window of a pâtisserie
on rue de Buci.

St. Louis and came directly upon the Brasserie de l'Ile St. Louis, where we had what was to be the first of many delicious steak *frites* we would enjoy there.

This brasserie conformed to the archetype in every respect: an interior of dark wood, a zinc-topped bar puddled with Pernod and pastis, and a lively, cigarette-waving clientele to whom unfiltered Gauloises and Gitanes were as oxygen. The place was always crowded, yet space would somehow always be found for new arrivals. Its atmosphere evoked foggy nights on the Seine, clandestine trysts, and mystery—I half-expected to see Jean Gabin coming through the door, for by now I had seen many French films, both new and old, in New York.

Two weeks later *Shakespeare Wallah* was shown in competition at the Berlin Festival. At the poorly attended press conference afterward Michel Delahaye, the critic from *Cahiers du Cinéma*, stood up and delivered a passionate homage to the film. For twenty minutes he spoke gratifyingly on what such a film meant to cinema and to the world, and when he had finished and sat down, he was replaced by the director Jean-Marie Straub, who delivered his own ovation. We could not follow any of their ringing pronouncements: we knew only that Delaheye liked the film and that he was seconded by Straub, who also wrote for *Cahiers*. We were incredibly excited and flattered by this response. *Cahiers du Cinéma* was then one of the most important film publications in the world: its founding members and regular critics included Truffaut and Godard, and the commentary and criticism of its pages had much influenced the development of contemporary film via the French New Wave.

This tribute was followed by an offer from the magazine's editors to pay for the translation and subtitling of *Shakespeare Wallah*, which they felt merited a release in France. The French instinctively recognize, encourage, and support talent regardless of nationality. They regard art as universal—it comes from everywhere and belongs to everyone. Jacques Robert, the owner of a French distribution company called Capital Films, had been so impressed by the film and its critical acclaim, which included a Best Actress award for Madhur Jaffrey from the Berlin Festival, that he offered to take it for distribution in France. This was to be a percentage arrangement, which meant the money would come later rather than up-front in the usual form of a minimum guarantee. We accepted his terms because we were still rather naive in the way of film business and, like all filmmakers, we wanted our film released and shown as quickly as possible.

Opposite: Merchant outside the Brasserie de l'Ile St. Louis with the proprietors, Marthe Guepratte and Michele Kappe, and the waiter, Ange "Gino" Allano.

Overleaf: The busy interior of the Brasserie de l'Ile St. Louis, a favorite hangout for writer James Jones during his Paris years and an important location for *A Soldier's Daughter Never Cries*.

Upon its release in France, *Shakespeare Wallah* received wonderful reviews and was a great success with audiences, doing very well for a subtitled film made by unknowns with an unknown cast. In 1968 it was voted the Best Foreign Film by the Académie du Cinéma, and we were invited to Paris to receive the award. The ceremony was held at Lasserre, a Michelin three-star restaurant of the most imposing refinement: Louis XVth-style paneled walls with inset paintings, soft lights, beautifully laid tables, and extravagant flower arrangements. This was my first experience of haute cuisine, cooking as an art form. Among the guests that night were the great French director Jacques Tati, the actor Michel Piccoli, and the English director Carol Reiss—all fellow recipients of a large crystal star in a red leather case. Room, guests, stars: all worked together to create the kind of glamour the French do so superbly, and which can be attributed to the attention they pay to every last detail of the setting, the company, and, of course, the meal itself. The meal we had that night was, like the occasion, unforgettable. It began with *pain de barbue*, poached salmon wrapped in fillets of brill served in a creamy white sauce, and this was followed by chicken cooked with truffles and wild rice. We had a salad of endive, avocado, and grapefruit, and then a dessert of sublime chocolate mousse covered in raspberry sauce and contained in little cups made of hard sugar with decorative sugar filaments forming a ribboned lid. We had never seen anything like this *fantaisie* of a dessert before, and we were loath to break into it. Each course was accompanied by an appropriate vintage wine, for Lasserre boasts one of the best cellars in Paris and is said to contain some 300,000 bottles of great wines collected since 1927. This meal marked my inauguration into classical French gastronomy.

→>‹←

Haute cuisine is the last remnant of a way of life that all but disappeared with the Second World War, of a time when chefs were encouraged to produce the most dazzling extravagant feasts. It is something above and beyond everyday cooking—it has its own vocabulary and strict principles, and it demands fierce dedication. It is predicated on using the very finest ingredients and creating sauces so subtle they defy even the most sophisticated palates to identify the constituents. Each course complements the next, blending textures, flavors, and colors to enchant the eye as well as the palate. Preparation can often take days,

Lasserre, a Michelin three-star restaurant on avenue Franklin Roosevelt. The discreet lettering and its veiled entranceway and windows serve as a model for luxurious French restaurants in New York and Beverly Hills.

A waiter sets up for the midday meal in Lasserre's main dining room.

Merchant lunching at Lasserre with actress Nathalie Richard and—avoiding the camera behind the waiter on the left—director/writer Andrew Litvack.

and thus this type of cooking is rarely found in the home—unless the home is affluent enough to afford one of the great chefs.

Haute cuisine is considered as much an art form as music, painting, or literature, and the French have long been acknowledged as masters of the métier. The great chefs are artists of the kitchen, and it is their talent, skill, and imagination that define this art. Many of these dishes have become classics, but the real reason haute cuisine survives is that every generation produces its own great chefs who create ever more inventive and brilliant ways of putting food together.

This style of cooking strives for perfection and consistency, and it is rewarded with Michelin stars, the greatest accolade a French restaurant can receive. French chefs have been known to shoot themselves if they lose a hard-won star bestowed by the Michelin Guide, the annual guidebook which rates every well-known restaurant in France.

→>-<←

In 1972 we made *Savages*, our first American film. It is one of our lesser-known works, although the claim might be made that over the years it has acquired something of a cult following. It was during the shooting of this film that we established the tradition of our Friday night post-wrap "curry party."

The budget for *Savages* was particularly lean, and the shooting conditions were correspondingly harsh. The cast of mostly Broadway and off-Broadway actors and the nonunion crew were working long hours, sometimes six-day weeks, for very meager wages. I wanted to do something to show my appreciation. We were shooting at Beechwood, a semi-abandoned neoclassical mansion in upstate New York, so I took up some bags of lentils and rice, some minced beef and chicken, and, using borrowed pots and pans, started the ritual of cooking for my cast and crew.

On that day's call sheet it was announced that I was hosting an Indian feast for everyone—at that time it was unprecedented that the producer of a film should cook supper for his cast and crew. I prepared *keema*, chicken cooked in yogurt, fragrant rice, lemon dal, with spiced cauliflower and potatoes. The evening was so successful, and the unit was so delighted by this gesture of solidarity from the producer, that I decided to repeat it the following week—and the week after that. More than thirty years later, at the week's end, I still take off my producer's hat, put on my chef's toque, and get to work in a borrowed kitchen. Everyone anticipates the

Anthony Korner, Ismail Merchant, and James Ivory in 1971 filming the dinner party for *Savages* in the Beechwood dining room.

22

"curry party," and if I failed to deliver I would probably have a mutiny on my hands.

Savages, with its surreal story, ambiguity, and fabulous imagery, was a film I was certain the French would respond to. I thought it would be ideal for the Cannes Film Festival, so I was surprised and disappointed when it was rejected. However, Pierre-Henri Deleau, who had established the Directors Fortnight at the festival, liked the film very much and selected it for that section. He must have liked it for the very same reasons the main festival probably turned it down: its offbeat story and cast, bizarre style, and absurdist tone. Though the film would not be in the main competition, we still had cause to celebrate because the Directors Fortnight is an important showcase for new directors.

On a mad whim I decided to celebrate the good news by inviting some friends to dinner at Maxim's before leaving for Cannes. Maxim's was then one of the most expensive restaurants in Paris and beyond our means, but it seemed an appropriate place to mark this occasion. Since opening in 1893, this restaurant has been associated with extravagance, glamour, and decadent high living—precisely the themes of *Savages*. At the time, Anthony Korner, a close friend who had been associate producer on *Savages* and who had designed the masks and grass costumes for the film's Mud People, was also in Paris. When I asked him to join us at Maxim's he thought I was joking.

Maxim's kitchen is said to have declined somewhat in recent years, though the restaurant is still well worth visiting for its fin de siècle ambience. The Art Nouveau interior of mahogany paneling, stained glass, palm trees, and elaborate architectural elements vividly evokes the spirit of its colorful past. But in 1972, the cuisine was still very haute indeed—and so were the prices. I didn't care. I felt like one of the plutocrats in *Savages* cavorting in white tie and tails, but with muddy bare feet. I was in high spirits and wanted to eat and dance and celebrate with my friends. We ordered the restaurant's signature dish: Sole Albert, sole dipped in butter and bread crumbs and baked in vermouth, named after Albert Blasser, the formidable maître d' who reigned over Maxim's in the 1930s. The bill that night for four people came to five hundred dollars. I can't imagine where I found the money to pay—I probably borrowed it from Tony Korner.

I had first met this charming urbane man in New York. Tony comes from a banking family, and they were—with good reason—alarmed when he dropped his career in banking to throw in his lot with Merchant Ivory, fashioning primitive mud masks, grass skirts, and conch bead G-strings for our film. He is now a successful publisher, and has remained a very good friend.

Tony would, of course, be coming with us to Cannes, together with Joe and Angelika Saleh, the principle investors in *Savages* and the earliest champions of our films, the script writers George Swift Trow and Michael O'Donague, various actors, assorted lords and ladies, and a maharaja, who caught flu as soon as he arrived. To accommodate the fifty-odd guests I had invited, we rented the Villa d'Andon in Grasse, a small, typically Provençal town in the hills above the Côte d'Azur. It is here where they grow the flowers whose oils are the essential ingredient of French scent—the hills are carpeted with lavender, mimosa, violet, jasmine, orange blossom, and rose. At night these sweetly intoxicating scents mingle and hang heavy in the dense warm air.

As our guests began to arrive in Grasse it quickly became clear I had overestimated the capacity of the villa and we had to take over a neighboring farmhouse, for every guest had brought someone. Joe, Jim, and I had intended to shoulder the expenses ourselves, but our money was running out fast. Joe pointed out to me that the cost of this *folie* of mine would soon rival the entire budget of *Savages*, and he proposed leaving a discreet note on the dining-room table asking everyone to make contributions toward the food. Unfortunately, the first person to see the note was Jim—and he was most upset about it. He thought it had been my idea, and he gave me a sharp lecture about how tacky it was to invite people to Cannes and then expect them to pay for the privilege. Joe, ever the canny financier, said he would be happy to remove the note if Jim was prepared to foot the bills himself. In the end, Joe, Jim, and I carried on sharing the bills.

Along with the villa we also found Rosa, a wonderful local cook whose generous size inspired confidence in her abilities. Every morning she would cycle to the villa bringing fresh croissants for our breakfast along with the ingredients for whatever she was planning to cook that day. In between the demands of the festival—the screenings, the parties, and the search for film distributors—I would join her in the kitchen in an attempt to learn some of the secrets of French, especially Provençal, cooking.

Rosa was fascinated by my methods, and I was intrigued by hers. I introduced her to fresh ginger and green chilies, which are used often and in great quantity in Indian cooking, but only rarely and sparingly, and as an exotic

addition, to French dishes. She introduced me to crème fraîche, a very adaptable, slightly sour cream, whose sharpness adds interest and depth to sauces and dressings. She would make coq au vin, explaining that the secret of the dish was in the quality of the wine. "Cooking won't disguise a bad wine, or turn it into a good wine. Start with inferior wine and you end up with an inferior dish. And the fowl must be a rooster because it has more flavor." She would frown as I tossed raw chilies liberally into her ratatouille, a Provençal vegetable stew, and then she would taste it and nod her approval. In return, she would add capers to my red mullet explaining that their tartness would bring out the sweetness of the fish. She was right. We traded recipes, secrets, and ideas, and each day the guests at the villa were the beneficiaries of these Indo–French dishes.

What amazed her most about my cooking, however, was its speed. I could whip up dinner for a dozen people in half an hour. Much as I love cooking, neither my lifestyle nor my temperament lends itself to hours of fussing in the kitchen. The French, on the other hand, think nothing of taking the best part of a week to prepare, for instance, a pheasant *pâtè en croûte*. So I was equally in awe at the patience of our cook who could happily spend what, to me, seemed like the whole day preparing a single magnificent dish.

✦✦✦

Every year at Cannes there are always a few films that unexpectedly create a buzz. No one knows how or why these particular films capture the collective imagination: they are not necessarily the films that win all the prizes, or the ones that are the most hyped, but they become the films everyone talks about and wants to see and be associated with. In 1972 one of these films was *Savages*. Its subject matter—the rise and fall of civilization during a weekend house party, no less—had caught the imagination of journalists and a younger audience, so that by the night the film appeared (this was the world premiere), every seat had been sold.

Only films in the main festival competition are shown at the Palais. The Directors Fortnight films are screened at various cinemas in the town, and *Savages* was to be shown at a small cinema on the rue d'Antibes. Given the size of the cinema and the number of people who wanted to see the film, pandemonium was inevitable. When we arrived, there were hundreds of people trying to get in. Among those still outside were some very important British film critics—

The garden side of the Villa d'Andon in Grasse, which, in 1972, was the first villa to house Merchant Ivory and guests at the Cannes Film Festival.

Kenneth Tynan, David Robinson, Derek Malcolm—so I manhandled them into the cinema. Penelope Houston, the editor of Britain's film journal *Sight and Sound*, was trapped between two glass doors and looked as though she was about to be crushed by the mob. I took her arm and yanked her in, and then they were all inside—battered and bruised, perhaps, but there, like the unflappable British characters in an adventure movie who have survived, say the Zulu rebellion, making wry jokes after a brush with death.

At Cannes every producer throws a party to celebrate the presence of his or her film at the festival, and I wanted to give a very special party at our villa. I arranged for Imrat Khan, one of India's leading sitar players, to play after dinner, which was to be prepared by the chefs from Gaylord, London's oldest Indian restaurant, who had driven from London to Cannes with all their equipment, basmati rice, and hard-to-find spices.

Everything had been carefully arranged for this event: handsome invitations had been sent out to the great, the good, and the useful of the festival, and transportation had even been provided to bring the guests from Cannes to Grasse. However, because of the buzz surrounding our film, this had become *the* party

A scene from *Savages* in which a tribe of Mud People—following a magic croquet ball through the forest—discovers a Pierce Arrow limosine on the grounds of a long-abandoned estate.

to be at that night and we were warned to expect gatecrashers. It had never occurred to me that we might need a bouncer; however, Tony Korner (who didn't exactly fit the bill as a strong-arm type) was assigned the job and he stationed himself by the gates of the villa. Anyone who arrived without an invitation was told in British tones of the most commanding authority that he or she would not be admitted and must, therefore, leave. This system worked surprisingly well until Louis Malle arrived without his invitation. We had met Malle when he was in Bombay making his documentary series *Phantom India* and we had become good friends. I happened to glance in the direction of the gates at the very moment Tony was getting rid of Malle. I rushed to Malle, embraced him, apologized for the misunderstanding, and ushered him in. "What are you *doing,*" I hissed at Tony, "turning away *Louis Malle?*" Tony didn't bat an eye. "No invitation, no party," he responded, upon which he abandoned his post and went to enjoy himself. Robert Altman and Andy Warhol, who had also forgotten their invitations, got in without any challenge.

The buffet supper of tandoori chicken, rice, and dal had been laid out in the dining room. I had arranged that the dessert, an Indian specialty called *jelabi,* which is a kind of sweet fritter, be served in the garden because watching the preparation is part of the fun. The chefs from Gaylord had brought their

Ultra Violet (otherwise known as Isabelle Collin-Dufresne), one of Andy Warhol's superstars (left), with actress Paulita Sedgwick (a distant cousin to Edie) in a scene from *Savages.* Once Ultra's character had been transformed from a Mud Person into a grand lady, she endeared herself to the crew and audience with the insouciance in which she wore her backless red satin evening gown back to front.

own tandoori oven with them for the chicken, and they also brought the huge iron cauldron in which the *jelabis* are cooked. They prepared the dough, dropped the pretzel-shaped pieces into the cauldron of sizzling oil, then doused the fried dough in honey syrup; these *jelabis* were eaten immediately, hot and sweet. The guests were delighted by this slick production-line process, and by the *jelabis* themselves. The chef pointed out a tall man who, he said, had eaten a dozen in one go; it was Robert Altman.

I was in an extraordinary situation: a producer of low-budget art-house films throwing the kind of extravagant party even the major studios might balk at. But it was worth it. The reviews for *Savages* were wonderful and even the party got reviewed. The French critics, perceiving it as a parable of American decadence, praised our far-out film, which had really started out as a lighthearted *jeu d' esprit,* and something of a dare. We also had enough interest from distributors to suggest that the expense of the party, if not the cost of making the film, might be recovered.

As there were a number of further screenings of *Savages* during the festival, all of which played to packed houses, we decided to go to one to see the audience's reaction. Everything was going well with the screening when suddenly, near the end, the screen was filled with images we had never seen before, including some semi-pornographic scenes from what appeared to be a Japanese film. Clearly the reels of another film had got mixed up with the reels of *Savages.* Tony Korner, whose French is fluent, ran into the projection room to find out what was going on. The projectionist shrugged and said that he ran the reels he was given and what was on those reels was no concern of his. It seemed to make no difference to the audience: *Savages* had passages with fake German ethnographic voice-over, and now there were scenes in Japanese. It was a film described as experimental, and not atypical of the Directors Fortnight. Perhaps, to some, the Japanese sex scenes gave our film a shot in the arm. When the lights went up, the audience did not seem displeased. We took the matter up with Pierre-Henri Deleau who organized a further screening of *Savages* as compensation, which meant that more distributors could see it. With the kind of attention *Savages* had attracted we never doubted for a moment that distributors would be rushing to offer us handsome deals. However, somehow no handsome deals materialized—the film was only shown sporadically in Paris, in a cinema on the Left Bank.

The Cannes of *Savages* was a very different experience from my first Cannes ten years earlier. Even though we were not in competition, our film drew the focus of the festival. I was no longer an outsider, a mere observer, but an active participant. We dressed up every night to go to parties and screenings. We explored the Côte d'Azur and sampled the excellent restaurants of the region. This was the Cannes I had heard stories about, the one I had always imagined. But my Cannes experience was not yet quite complete—I had not yet walked up the red-carpeted staircase of the Palais, admitted to the main competition, arm in arm with my stars. That was still to come.

Savages had established a Merchant Ivory presence at Cannes, and we had found a formula that would work well in the years to come: rent a handsome villa outside town; fill it with our actors, writers, cameramen, editors, and friends; give a number of parties, culminating in the biggest one on the night of the film's presentation; and, of course, have as much fun as possible.

→>·<←

As our films gradually found a market in France, I began to spend more and more time there and became increasingly attracted to the French way of life. The French work hard, but there is a strong element of hedonism in their nature. Their pursuit of pleasure, their admiration of fine things, and their appreciation of quality is evident and explicit in the way they live: in their homes, their dress and, above all, their attitude toward food.

France has a thriving restaurant culture: In no other country in the world have I seen so many restaurants always filled with people passionately eating, drinking, and enjoying themselves, or simply sitting outside sipping a coffee and liqueur. The term alfresco may be Italian, but the French seem to have made this practice all their own. From the earliest days of spring until well after the first frosts begin to bite, Paris—as well as every other French city, town, and village—becomes one vast restaurant as tables and chairs sprout up on every sidewalk. Even Lasserre, which doesn't go as far as littering the avenue Franklin Roosevelt with outdoor furniture, has a retractable roof so its customers can dine under the stars without any loss of ambience.

A French evening out always begins with a spirited debate about where to eat. The choice is governed not by location or fashion, as is often the case in, say,

Overleaf: La Palette is virtually the sole traditional outdoor café on the Left Bank that has escaped the installation of ugly glass partitions reaching out onto the sidewalk. This modernizing fad separates the tables from the crowd walking by—to old-timers this convivial mingling seemed the whole idea. La Palette is therefore much in demand by movie makers hoping to evoke the Paris that was.

New York or London, but rather by the kind of food everyone feels like eating. And when everyone has agreed on whether they want haute cuisine, *cuisine paysanne, cuisine bourgeois*, a regional cuisine, or just simple steak *frites*, they choose the restaurant that perfectly matches their expectations and their mood. It might also be a Vietnamese, Italian, Lebanese, or North African restaurant, for, as in New York and London, there is a wonderful assortment of foreign cuisines from which to choose in Paris. Locals know which restaurants specialize in particular dishes, which prepare them the best, which have the best wine cellars, and which are to be avoided because the chef is going through a rough patch. And the French also know there is no problem, no disagreement, and no situation that cannot be resolved over a good meal.

The function of food as a diplomatic tool was a French attitude I first became aware of when I had to confront Jacques Robert over the outstanding money we thought he owed us for our film *Shakespeare Wallah*, a film he had taken for distribution and with which had done very well. Jacques Robert was a colorful man devoted to cinema; but his partner, a bearded and bearlike Russian named Gorovich, hated parting with money. Their way of dealing with this situation was to invite Jim and me to lunch. They took us to the Closerie de Lilas in Montparnasse, where we dined on foie gras with special truffles found only in the south of France and hunted, we were informed, by a particular kind of boar, not pig. Monsieur Gorovich, who had plump, rounded, white hands, ordered as an entrée an extraordinary-looking white trussed sausage full of delectable juices. He attacked it with gusto, waving about the sharp knife used for cutting the strings in such a way that, to our eyes, it looked as if he were about to eat his own hands. Bottle after bottle of champagne was ordered, but when we broached business, they regretted that they had no money to pay us. The best we could get from them was the return of the rights to the film.

Robert had also distributed another of our films, *Autobiography of a Princess*, and again Jim and I had to pursue him for the money he owed us—we needed it to buy our tickets back home. We pleaded with him remorsefully until he eventually arranged for us to collect the money directly from the woman who owned the cinema where the film had played. This woman, a proprietor of art houses on the Left Bank and in the Marais, also owned a string of pornographic cinemas in the red-light district of Pigalle, which is where we were told we could find her. She was not there when we arrived and the box-office clerk hospitably offered us tickets to the film. We said we would wait outside. The owner eventually arrived carrying a brown paper bag, which she thrust into our hands. Jim and I looked in the bag. There was enough money to pay for our passage home: over two thousand dollars in francs.

However, getting money out of a distributor could be, as we discovered with *Autobiography of a Princess*, the least of our difficulties. That film is only an hour in length, and in order to release it in commercial cinemas in France we decided to run it with the half-hour *Helen, Queen of the Nautch Girls*. We sent the only negative of the latter film to Laboratoires CTM in Paris. But, instead of making a print, the laboratory impounded the negative—apparently the French distributor owed a great deal of money to this laboratory, and they decided to hold our negative hostage until he paid up. It took more than a year to resolve this dispute with the laboratory, at the end of which the *Helen* negative disappeared entirely and was found again only by chance in 1998.

But, just when the French are at their most exasperating, when you throw up your hands and vow never to have any more dealings with them, they will do something that once again sends them soaring in your estimation. In 1976 we were planning to make *Roseland*, a film about the famous dance hall in New York and the characters who frequented it. Our idea sounded vague to financiers and we were having difficulties raising the initial development money when we were advised to try the Institut National Audiovisual in Paris. This seemed like a long shot because the film had little connection to, or seeming relevance for, France—it was about an old American institution. But I applied and was astonished and delighted when I.N.A. committed twenty thousand dollars to the project, which allowed us to go ahead with a script. The French supported the film because they felt the idea had merit: the nationality of its subject matter was immaterial.

The French again demonstrated their contempt for national boundaries in terms of the arts when our film *The Europeans* was selected as the British entry at the Cannes Film Festival in 1979. I was delighted to have a feature film in competition at Cannes at last, but the Association of British Film Producers felt quite different about the matter. They told us that since neither the film's producer nor director was British, it could not be given British nationality. My first reaction to this was disbelief. Although *The Europeans* was an adaptation of the

Henry James novel and had been shot in America, the film was largely financed by Britain's National Film Finance Corporation. In addition, Ruth Jhabvala, the scriptwriter, had grown up in England and held a British passport, while Henry James, although an American by birth, had become a British citizen in his later years. The crew on the film had been largely British, with British actors, such as Robin Ellis, in the leading roles. But the Association of British Film Producers was adamant—they did not want *The Europeans* as a British entry, even though it would be the *only* British film in competition at Cannes that year.

Letters flew back and forth and the issue was debated in the press—finally the Cannes selection committee put an end to the dispute by declaring that it was up to them to decide what nationality a film should bear, and they had decided *The Europeans* was British. Such was the pique of the English staff of the Association of British Film Producers over this that they resisted displaying the poster of the film at their booth in Cannes, and would tear it down at night.

So we were back in Cannes, this time in competition. I finally walked up the red-carpeted staircase of the Palais arm in arm with my stars, including the late Lee Remick, and it was every bit as thrilling as I had imagined. *The Europeans* won no prizes, but the film marked a significant breakthrough for us in that it was taken for distribution by Gaumont, one of the largest distributors in France. Often over the years, when I had been in Paris walking along the Champs Élysées, I had looked at the huge billboards of the many cinemas lining the street and wondered if one of our films would ever play there. Now it seemed to me that our days of backstreet art-house cinemas were over.

To celebrate the occasion, Gaumont threw a party for us at their elaborate villa, which was generously staffed with liveried butlers, bartenders, chefs, and chauffeurs. We, on the other hand, had taken a rather small villa in Juan les Pins where we entertained in our own way: Connie Kaiserman, the associate producer of *The Europeans*, acted as hostess, while I served as butler, bartender, chef, and chauffeur. This, of course, was in addition to my official job as producer, which, during the festival, meant trying to get as many people as possible to see the film, as many distributors as possible to buy it, and as much publicity for it as I could possibly generate.

There was much to be said for our way of doing things. One of the great attractions of our modest villa was that it was located next to a farm, and each day the farmer would bring us his homegrown vegetables and melons. I greatly appreciated our neighbor's freshly grown gifts, which I would use to supplement the bounty from my daily forage in the local open-air market. I also benefitted from the garden of our little villa, which was a charming mix of vegetables, grape vines, and flowers, with roses next to the carrots and daisies amidst the lettuce.

The south of France was settled first by the Greeks, and then the Romans, and today it still seems to have more in common with these Mediterranean cousins than with the northern half of the country. The land, the climate, and the fiery, passionate, Latin temperament of its people all speak of the full-blooded spirit of southern Europe. So, too, does the food, which is predicated on the simple, uncomplicated preparation of the freshest ingredients rather than on the complex, precise principles of haute cuisine. My commitments during the festival meant that I never had enough time to explore Provence in any great depth, but I came to know much about it through the food markets and the restaurants of the seaside towns.

The markets here are a gold mine for the cook: They sell every kind of fresh vegetable, all grown locally, with pride of place given to tomatoes, onions, and

Merchant waiting to buy the very fresh, succulent vegetables in the rue de Buci market.

A view of the rue de Buci market, near Merchant's apartment in the 6th arrondissement.

garlic—the key ingredients of Provençal cooking. Bell peppers, asparagus, green beans, zucchini, aubergines, artichokes, and fennel, which grows wild everywhere and even flavors pastis, the local firewater, are featured prominently in the dishes of the region. Then there is the abundance of ripe, aromatic fruit from the local orchards: peaches, apricots, plums, cherries, figs, persimmons, quinces, citrus fruits, and melons, especially the tiny, juicy Cavaillon melons that can only be found in this part of France.

In the meat market there is lamb that has been raised in the alpine region of Alpes–de–Haute–Provence and fed on wild herbs, which give the meat its distinctive and subtle flavor. But, as a devoted fish-eater, it was the fish stalls to which I was always drawn first. The variety of fish that flourish in these waters is astonishing: everything from tiny succulent sardines to fat sea bass, and all manner of shellfish—mussels and oysters, sea urchins and clams—as well as squid, cuttlefish, and octopus. Fish is the great staple of the Mediterranean kitchen, and the fish stalls were always crowded and noisy with stallholders shouting out the names of the fish on sale and with shoppers keenly inspecting and buying. The lively, vibrant atmosphere reminded me of the fish markets back home in Bombay that I used to visit as a boy with my father, who knew how to spot the freshest fish and the best bargains.

My greatest discoveries in Provence were herbs and olives, neither of which is used in Indian cooking. Provence is famous for its herbs, which are cultivated throughout the region: basil for *pistou* (the local variation of Italian pesto), which is the principle ingredient of the local favorite *soupe au pistou*, as well as oregano, marjoram, rosemary, thyme, mint, chervil, savory, and many others. These herbs are found in every garden, grow wild everywhere, and can be bought either fresh or dried in the markets where their potent smells fill the air. A specific combination of these, known as Herbes de Provence is sold in little clay pots. Open one in the middle of a New York winter and the heady scent immediately transports you back to this land of sun and sea and blue skies.

The outdoor market on rue de Buci features a variety of fresh fish (top), shellfish (center), and mushrooms (bottom).

Olive trees grow everywhere in Provence and olive oil is the chief cooking medium. A combination of climate and late harvesting produces an oil that is full flavored and low in acidity, and is therefore considered one of the finest in the world. The markets have whole stalls entirely devoted to the many varieties of olive: tiny ones no bigger than raisins; huge ones almost the size of plums;

some marinated in herbs, some in olive oil, others in brine; black ones, brown ones, green ones, reddish ones. Olives are the main ingredient of *tapenade*, a local paste made of black olives, garlic, capers, anchovies, lemon juice, and olive oil that is spread on slices of toasted baguette.

Due to the experimental nature of the way I cook, I am always attracted to ingredients that are unfamiliar to me. When I have no idea how they should be used, I improvise and come up with some very unexpected flavors. I love to intrigue my guests by combining ingredients in ways they don't expect. For example, I smear *pistou* over fish before grilling or baking it, and also use the paste as an unusual way of seasoning vegetables and meat.

Fortunately, my first serious excursions into the French kitchen took place on the Côte d'Azur, where the Mediterranean influence on the local Provençal cuisine invites variation and adaptation. The French always seemed to find my subcontinental interpretations of their cuisine quite diverting and interesting. Over the years I have succeeded in putting all the classic Provençal dishes, from *salade Niçoise* to ratatouille, under the influence of chilies, ginger, cumin, and coriander, without offending purists.

→>-<-

Jim had read a number of books by Jean Rhys, most of which were set in Paris, and had become an admirer of her work. Ruth Jhabvala, our scriptwriter, was equally enthusiastic about Rhys's work, although she was rather doubtful that it would adapt well to film. But we were keen to make a film in France, so there was, perhaps, a certain inevitability about our next project. Jim was particularly taken with *Quartet*, Rhys's semiautobiographical account of her relationship with the writer Ford Madox Ford during the 1920s in Paris, and he felt this novel could make a fine film. Despite her misgivings about the project, Ruth wrote the screenplay and we began to consider actresses for the part of Marya, the heroine. Isabelle Adjani had been brilliant in Truffaut's film *L'Histoire d'Adèle H.* and we were thinking about contacting her when *she* got in touch with us about a possible collaboration on another Rhys novel, *The Wide Sargasso Sea.* I flew to Paris and met with her to see whether she would consider doing *Quartet* instead, and, as this film provided her with an equally strong leading role, she was receptive to the idea. I arranged a telephone call between

Jim and Isabelle, which for some reason took place from a phone booth while Jim was shopping at Saks Fifth Avenue in New York.

As this was to be an Anglo–French coproduction I needed to find a French coproducer. Through a friend of Connie Kaiserman, I was introduced to Humbert Balsan, a French producer of documentaries who, together with his partner Jean-Pierre Mahot de la Querantonnais, now wanted to become involved in feature films. I arranged to meet Humbert for breakfast at the Marriott Hotel at Porte Maillot. All I knew about him was that he came from a wealthy bourgeois family. Our meeting went very well, and by the end I was absolutely certain that this savvy sweet-talking charmer would make an excellent coproducer—he had made no attempt to pick up the tab for breakfast. Clearly he knew the value of money, and *I* knew we would get on well.

Humbert's mother lived in the 1st arrondissement near the Bristol Hotel. In the courtyard of her apartment block she had a small studio that was usually occupied by Humbert's nephew, who happened to be away at that time. Due to our budget restrictions, Humbert offered me the studio to live in during the film's preproduction period. Humbert accepted the economical principles of Merchant Ivory filmmaking; in fact, he shared them. This arrangement had the added advantage of affording me the opportunity to live among the French in a family environment—a privilege the very private French people rarely afford strangers. As the studio had a minute kitchen, we ate out a lot, and would often end up at the Bar des Théâtres on the avenue Montaigne just opposite the Théâtre des Champs Élysées. This place was popular with the post-theater crowd, and also with Humbert because the head waiter, who sported a lush walrus moustache, came from Carcassonne in southern France, where Humbert was also from, so we were always given special attention.

Britain's National Film Finance Corporation had put up the development money for *Quartet*, and we had commitments from the distributor Gaumont, as well as Roger Corman's New World Pictures in Los Angeles. But there was still a shortfall in our 1.8-million-dollar budget. Twentieth Century Fox was interested in the project, but we were waiting for their final decision. For a week Humbert and I sat by the phone, getting more and more anxious, until we finally got the call from Fox we were hoping for, and with it our completed budget.

Now that we were certain the film was really going to be made, I needed to

Opposite, above: A scene from *Quartet*, shot in the doorway of Prunier, a Parisan restaurant. Left to right: Wiley Wood as Cairn; Isabelle Adjani as Marya Zelli; and Alan Bates as H. J. Heidler, the character Jean Rhys modeled on writer Ford Madox Ford.

Opposite, below: La Palette again, in a scene from *Quartet*. The Pornographer, played by Pierre Clementi, is ever on the lookout for likely young women to cast in his films.

find a more permanent temporary home in Paris. Happily, an in-law of Humbert's had an unoccupied apartment on rue Jean Goujon near the Rond-Point des Champs Élysées, which I was able to rent for six months. This apartment block was next door to the San Regis, a very charming small hotel with an aura of privacy and exclusivity, and it became home to our two English stars, Maggie Smith and Alan Bates.

One of the great advantages of living in this area was that it was only a short stroll to the Champs Élysées with its many fine restaurants. The Bar des Théâtres, especially, was one of our regular haunts during filming. Though I rarely had the foresight to make a reservation, the affable red-blazered waiters would somehow manage to squeeze us into one of the tightly packed tables. The menu was short and simple: roasted meats and chicken, grilled steak and fish, and the best *pommes frites* in Paris. If we were in a hurry, the waiters would make sure we were fed briskly; on more leisurely occasions, such as a Sunday lunch, we could linger as long as we liked despite the crush at the bar waiting for a table. Being more of a brasserie in style than a restaurant with rigid hours, the bar was happy to feed us at the oddest times without making a fuss. Maggie and Alan enjoyed it because it was a place to relax, even though we often had to raise our voices to be heard above the clatter of dishes and conversations—but both are famously good at that.

Many of the scenes in *Quartet* were set in restaurants, and during our location scouting we visited dozens to find ones that were right in terms of period and atmosphere. One that we considered was Bofinger in rue de la Bastille. Established in 1864, Bofinger claims to be the oldest brasserie in Paris, and is now listed as a historic monument. Its founder Frederic Bofinger came from Alsace and is credited with introducing draught beer to the capital. The restaurant was completely remodeled in 1918 in the reigning Art Nouveau style of the period, and this is the style that survives today. It certainly has one of the most striking interiors of any restaurant I have visited: no one could fail to be impressed by the soaring stained-glass dome and sweeping brass-railed staircase. Decorative marquetry and tile panels add to the splendor of this place. Bofinger is famous for its *choucroute*, which, unlike the sharply acidic sauerkraut of Germany, has a very gentle, delicate flavor. Many celebrities have been regular visitors over the years, not because Bofinger is fashionable—indeed, this area was in decline until its revival in the 1980s when the Bastille opera was built—but simply because they love the food. The menu favors specialties from Alsace including an unusual fish *choucroute*, which is so popular that more than a thousand are served every week. Although we eventually decided against using Bofinger as a location for *Quartet*, we frequently feasted there, and still do.

One restaurant we did use in the film was Polidor on rue Monsieur le Prince, in the 6th arrondissement near the Sorbonne. A long-established favorite of professors and students from the university, it was one of Ernest Hemingway's Latin Quarter haunts and it still retains its original late-Victorian interior.

There was a long line of people waiting for tables when Humbert and I went to sample this restaurant, and he told me it was always like this. When we were finally seated, we were rewarded and revived by glasses of *kir*—the delicious drink of chilly white wine with a dash of blackcurrant liqueur—which the maître d' offers her customers to invigorate them after their long wait. We dined on *confit de canard*, goose prepared in its own fat, which is a native dish of Gascony, one of the great gastronomic regions of France and one that is famous for its goose and duck. This is where foie gras, a French specialty, comes from—traditionally eaten at the start of a meal, it is usually accompanied by a glass of the sweet white wine of Sauternes or Barsac. Gascony's neighboring areas of Périgord and Quercy are the largest producers of that most prized ingredient of French cooking, the black truffle, a subterranean fungus so rare and costly it is known as "the black diamond." As truffles are rumored to be dug up from the earth by pigs—I have never verified this story—they are perhaps not quite kosher for a good Muslim; but it would be churlish on my part not to try one of France's greatest delicacies.

One of the key scenes in *Quartet* takes place in a nightclub, and we re-created the legendary decadent atmosphere of Parisian nightlife in the 1920s at Le Boeuf-sur-le-Toit, a restaurant-cum-nightclub in rue du Colisée, just off the Champs Élysées. The origins of this nightclub go back to the beginning of the century, although over the years it has gone through a variety of names and locations, taking its present title from a musical written by one of its chief patrons, Jean Cocteau. In 1941 the restaurant moved to its present site, a converted small theater that was built for the dancer Isadora Duncan. The Art Deco interior is modeled on the style of a transatlantic liner of the 1920s and, despite some later

The entrance to Bofinger, a brasserie on rue de la Bastille. At right, the rich Art Nouveau interior of Bofinger.

Restaurant Polidor, one of the many locations in which *Quartet* was filmed. At right, the interior of Polidor, taken during a quiet moment before the restaurant opens for the day.

superficial additions, most of its period detail was exactly right for our purposes. It had an authentic feel that our art department could build on, and its size made it practical for filming.

For a guide to how these scenes should look, we drew on the images of the great French photographer Lartigue, who left a wonderful record of that midnight world and the people who inhabited it. Lartigue, in his nineties but still spry and humorous, visited the set while we were shooting, and took some delightfully wry and witty photographs of the 1920s world we had created. His small, well-worn camera surprised our cinematographer Pierre Lhomme, an artist whose images magically create the particular texture of a specific location and time with an infallible accuracy.

As jazz had been all the rage in twenties' Paris, we used American musicians for performers at our club (we did not call it Le Boeuf-sur-le-Toit). We wanted to cast Nell Carter, who had been so impressive in the New York musical *Ain't Misbehavin'*, as our featured singer, but our shooting dates clashed with her other commitments. However, a touring company of *Ain't Misbehavin'* was performing in Paris and one night Jim and I, together with Richard Robbins, who composes the music for all our films, went to see it. Armelia McQueen, in Nell Carter's role, was sensational, and we managed to persuade her and some of the show's musicians to perform in our nightclub scene, playing new jazz songs that Dick Robbins wrote for the film.

The first day's shooting of *Quartet* took place at a village church in the countryside near Paris. In India it is traditional to begin a film by garlanding the camera with flowers and handing out sweetmeats to everyone on the set. This ritual is meant to bring good fortune to the production and is one I always try to observe wherever we are working. However, shooting was to begin at eight in the morning, and I had no idea where I could find Indian sweets and garlands in Paris at dawn. Jean-Pierre Mahot, my coproducer, suggested chocolates as a substitute. As for garlands, well, assuming we could find any flowers at all so early in the morning, I would have to weave them into a garland myself because, as Jean-Pierre pointed out, there simply wasn't much demand for Indian garlands in Paris. We found a *chocolatier* and a florist in a tiny village nearby and made it to the location with only minutes to spare. I hung my hastily strung garland over the Panaflex camera and rushed around offering chocolates

Armelia McQueen singing in the nightclub scene in *Quartet*, shot on the site of the legendary Paris nightclub of the 20s Le Boeuf-sur-le-Toit.

to everyone, explaining our Indian traditions as I went. "Yes, yes," I was told, "but here in France we mark the occasion with champagne at the end of the first day." "Fine," I replied, "we will observe the French tradition also, but for now *please* take a bite of the chocolate, it will bring us good luck."

I was soon to discover that first-day champagne was only one of many French rituals to be observed. Meal times, of course, were sacrosanct and had to comprise two courses, followed by cheese and dessert and accompanied by wine. If the director wanted to work beyond the specified shooting time, he had to obtain the agreement of the entire unit. This was never easy as it meant the French crew would miss their nightly family dinner, also a ritual. Shooting on a Sunday morning was out of the question as it would clash with Sunday mass, another ritual, and, more important, with Sunday lunch. In these ways the French reminded me very much of the Bengalis in India, who also live a ritual-istic way of life.

My knowledge of French rituals and customs was increasing the more time I spent in France, but there were still times when some unfamiliar rite caught me unawares. One such occasion occurred during the shooting of *Quartet*, when the Indian filmmaker Satyajit Ray paid a visit to Paris. We had known Ray since 1962 when we made our first film, *The Householder*, and we had remained close ever since.

Ray's work was regarded highly in France, and Jean-Pierre Mahot gave a dinner at his mother's apartment in Ray's honor. Maggie Smith and Alan Bates were also invited to this somewhat formal affair, where everything had been done with the greatest style and elegance. It was a spectacular evening: the very tall Ray sitting regally in his white *kurta* and shawl with Maggie Smith beside him making witty conversation rather desperately, for, though the keenest observer one could ever hope to meet, Ray's supply of small talk was rationed carefully.

The sumptuous dinner began with *crevettes* on a bed of salad in a classic vinaigrette. Then the main course appeared: a huge pheasant, elaborately gar-nished and dressed in its flowing plumes, its dead, beady eyes staring. It was borne into the dining room on a silver tray, and presented to Ray with great ceremony. "My dear," said Maggie Smith to me, "whatever could it be? Do you suppose it's one of Judy's *chapeaux*?" (Judy Moorcroft was our costume designer on the film.) Ray looked at me with questioning eyes. What, he appeared to be asking, was he expected to do with it? I had no idea. What *was* he expected to do with it? Bless it? Distribute it to the guests? After a few more moments during which our bewilderment grew, the pheasant was ceremoniously borne away. We learned later that it is a French custom to present the main course to the guest of honor before it is served. It reappeared soon minus its plumage—this time it came sliced and accompanied with a wild-mushroom sauce, crisp *pommes Lyonnais*, and green beans. We ended the meal with *frais du bois* (wild strawberries), which were all the more appreciated as they were out of season, served with a sweet *crème Chantilly*.

Pandit Ram Narain, the Indian *sarangi* player, happened to be in Paris to play a concert and was another guest that night. After dinner he and his tabla player entertained us with their music. Ray explained the mood of the raga, an ancient traditional melodic pattern in Indian music, and described its intricacies. Most people there that night had never experienced Indian classical music, and Ray and the other Indians present, including myself, had never experienced a meal of this kind in an aristocratic French home. The standards of both the music and the dinner were impeccable, similar in their rigor and fastidiousness, and similarly based on ancient traditions. Both arts, that of pleasing the palate and that of pleasing the ear, are devotional. For many Indians, the raga enters into the sphere of the spiritual, of religious feelings. For most French, the celebration of food and the serious enjoyment of nature's bounty is a way of paying respect to the old gods, especially Ceres, goddess of plenty.

During shooting, Friday nights were reserved for our curry parties, of which, at first, the French crew didn't know what to make. A producer cooking for his unit was extremely unusual in itself, and odder still was the idea of an Indo–French feast. I had cooked for French friends and colleagues before, mostly in Cannes, and they had been intrigued by, and appreciative of, my hybrid cooking. But the crew of *Quartet* would be my first nonpartisan critics. I had recently discovered what was perhaps the only common link between Indian and French cooking—mustard—and I decided to make it the theme of the first crew dinner. Mustard seeds are used as often in Indian cooking as prepared mustard is used in French food. The French city of Dijon, in Burgundy, calls itself the mustard capital of the world, and produces the classic Dijon mustard as well as many flavored varieties.

Above: A pâtisserie on rue de Buci.

Below: Ismail Merchant, Andrew Litvack, and James Ivory in the rue de Buci market.

The chief principle of my cooking is that it be easy to prepare and quick to cook. After working all day I don't want to spend the whole evening fussing over food, and when I have guests coming straight from the set I know they will be tired and hungry and will need to be fed quickly. I rarely go to the market with a shopping list—I prefer to see what looks good in the market and then decide what to make. On that day, the fish stall was shining with succulent sardines, so I prepared fresh sardines with Dijon mustard, mustard seeds, and tarragon; as well as chicken with tarragon mustard, fresh tarragon, and cayenne pepper; and green beans, dal, and rice. For dessert I bought the ripest fruit in the market: strawberries, cherries, kiwi, peaches, and apples, to combine with a bottle of good Beaujolais.

Crowds of people came to our dinner party that night, not only the crew, but no one was turned away—whoever they were, we never found out. Some, perhaps, were friends of Isabelle's. Luckily I had cooked enough, and had bought enough wine. However, the triumph of the evening was not that there was enough to go around: For me, the great triumph of the evening was that the French crew members were overwhelming in their praise for my food, and demanded to know when I would cook for them again.

✦➤◄✦

One of the great pleasures of making *Quartet* was the chance to live in Paris as an inhabitant, albeit a temporary one, rather than merely a visitor. I was able to indulge my passion for shopping, cooking, and entertaining friends. (When I say shopping I do not mean anything but shopping for food. I never shop otherwise. Browsing for clothes is something I do when I can't shop for food, or when I'm bored.) The landmarks of the city that most visitors want to see first are the Eiffel Tower, the Arc de Triomphe, and Notre Dame—and now the glass pyramid in the court of the Louvre. But, from my earliest visits, I was always drawn to the great food market of Les Halles. Unfortunately, however, the market was moved from the center of Paris in the early 1970s. The congestion and traffic generated by such a huge wholesale market in the center of Paris eventually became too much and, like Covent Garden market in London, it was moved to the outskirts of the city. With that move I feel Paris lost some of its vitality and character.

The scale of Les Halles was quite simply monumental. The buzzing hustle

and bustle, the frantic vibrant activity, and the inexhaustible energy of the retailers reminded me very much of Crawford Market, which is the biggest in Bombay, but a mere speck compared to Les Halles. Here were *acres* of fruit and vegetables of every kind from every region of France; as well as poultry and game from Perigord; lamb from the Basque country and the much-prized *pré-salé* lamb from the salty marshlands of Brittany; and the famous Charolais beef from Burgundy—it was endless.

I would walk around Les Halles all day, constantly discovering new things, and never getting tired. Sometimes I would stop at one of the many restaurants that fringed the market area for something to eat. It was on one of my earliest visits here that I first tasted crème brûlée, a dessert of set vanilla custard covered with a brittle caramel that you shatter with a spoon. As with every other French dish, crème brûlée may vary from region to region: In Provence, the custard is flavored with orange; in the Dordogne, where walnut trees flourish, the regional variation incorporates chopped walnuts. If I were to make it myself I might try flavoring the custard with almonds or pistachios or cardamoms.

No matter where you may live in Paris, you are never very far from an open-air market full of fresh produce and, often, a smorgasbord of regional specialties. In addition, every *quartier* supports a range of the food shops that are considered essential in France: a high quality greengrocer selling every variety of fruit and vegetable; a *boulangerie* giving off tempting aromas of freshly baked bread; a pâtisserie displaying elegantly presented fruit tarts, elaborate cakes, and tiny petits fours. There will also be a butcher, whose job is not just to sell meat, but to prepare each cut individually for his customers according to the specific dish they intend to make, and a fishmonger, who does the same thing with his various cuts of fish. Then there is that savior of busy lives, the charcuterie, with its enormous stock of cooked meats, salamis, hams, endless varieties of pâté, jars of cassoulet, savory pies and tarts, spit-roasted chickens, and various salads—all made on the premises. I have never shopped in a charcuterie without always buying more than I intended, because, not only does everything look fresh and delicious, it is always presented in a most enticing and irresistible way.

Feasting in France also means feasting on the incredible varieties of ethnic foods available: Indian, Lebanese, Moroccan, Greek, Italian, Thai, and Japanese. And, perhaps because this is Paris, these foreign delicacies often seem more

Heaped up delicacies in a charcuterie window on rue de Buci. In the foreground are fresh stuffed snails, ready to go into the oven, and a variety of pâtés.

delicious, more carefully prepared, and more aesthetically pleasing than they might elsewhere, as if they were competing with French food.

The standards of all these shops, foreign or French, are consistently high because the baker and his colleagues know that it's only a short walk to the neighboring *quartier* with its own food shops, and that is where his customers will go if he fails them. The French will not tolerate second-rate food; they want the best and are willing to pay for it, as I once discovered in the south of France. I had just bought some lamb for a lamb curry, and as I wandered around the market I came upon a stall selling mushrooms. Countless types of mushrooms are eaten in France and I was still discovering varieties that were new to me. This stall had some unfamiliar mushrooms so, of course, I wanted to try them. I thought I would throw them into the curry as their texture would make an interesting contrast to the lamb. I asked for a kilo, and the stallholder asked for five hundred francs—a hundred dollars. I froze. "A hundred dollars for *mushrooms?*" I asked in disbelief. "Cèpes," replied the stallholder, "special seasonal mushrooms from Gascony." And did people really pay hundreds of dollars for mushrooms? I wondered. The stallholder indicated the queue forming behind me. Evidently they did.

During the time we were shooting *Quartet* I continued to explore the restaurants, and it never ceased to amaze me that after nearly two decades of making regular visits to France I could still open a menu and find classic dishes that were new to me. This is partly because the French are so much more inventive than anyone else—they must have a hundred ways of preparing potatoes—but also because of the diversity of the regional cuisines, each one based on local produce. Even where ingredients overlap between one region and another, their methods of preparation can be entirely different. The Mediterranean cooking of the south contrasts in every possible way to the cooking of the north where butter, cream, and dairy products feature strongly. In Burgundy and Bordeaux, the chief wine-growing regions of France, wine is an essential element in many dishes. And so it continues, each region with a well-defined and extensive cuisine of its own. Perhaps Charles de Gaulle, the president of France from 1958 to 1969, summed it up best in an interview he once gave to *Newsweek*. "How," he asked rhetorically, "can you be expected to govern a country that has two hundred and forty-six kinds of cheese?"

When *Quartet* was selected for competition at Cannes in 1981, we rented a glorious jasmine-covered villa in Antibes, called the Villa de la Garoupe, which had a large and beautiful flower-filled garden and, located as it was right on the bay, a picture-postcard view of the rocky cliffs leading down to the cobalt-blue sea. The villa was long, narrow, and high. Its rooms were strung out like beads on a string, so that most of them looked out on the garden on one side, and the seacoast, stretching east, on the other. It was luxurious and French, understated in its decoration, with plain white walls and dark-beamed ceilings. But it also felt English in a way—like an English country house, and we learned that Pamela Harriman, the American ambassador to France, had lived there for years. It was also the subject of some sinister stories, such as one that during World War II, prisoners had been interrogated there. But these shadows were dispelled by the bright sun and blue sky and blue water.

This promised to be our most exciting visit yet to Cannes: We had a really strong French-based film in competition with three internationally famous movie stars, including the French box-office magnet Isabelle Adjani. So we were very disappointed to learn that both Maggie Smith and Alan Bates had other professional commitments at that time and would be unable to attend the festival. Then we heard that Isabelle Adjani would not be coming either. She gave us no reason for this, but her absence was all the more surprising because, in addition to *Quartet*, she had another film in competition, Andrei Zulloski's *Obsession*. She had an aversion to the press and publicists even then, and over the years it has grown, so that now she is rarely seen at these kinds of events. Her absence would be a great blow for us. Actors of the magnitude we had in *Quartet* are a great attraction to the press and photographers, and when a producer is lucky enough to have a film with stars, he welcomes all the publicity they generate. And we had three; but they could not—or would not—be there.

Quartet was well received by the press and audiences, and we began to hear rumors that Isabelle was the favorite for the best-actress award. Cannes is always awash with such rumors, so we didn't pay much attention until we were given an official indication—a kind of discreet hint by the festival organizers—that, indeed, this particular rumor might be true. With that, Isabelle decided to attend the ceremony, and she collected the best-actress award, sharing it between her two films. She came to the villa with a great many friends in tow, as a star should on her victory night, and the party went on until very late. We

Above: Isabelle Adjani and Alan Bates in the nightclub scene in *Quartet.*

Below: Marya Zelli (Isabelle Adjani) visiting her husband in prison.

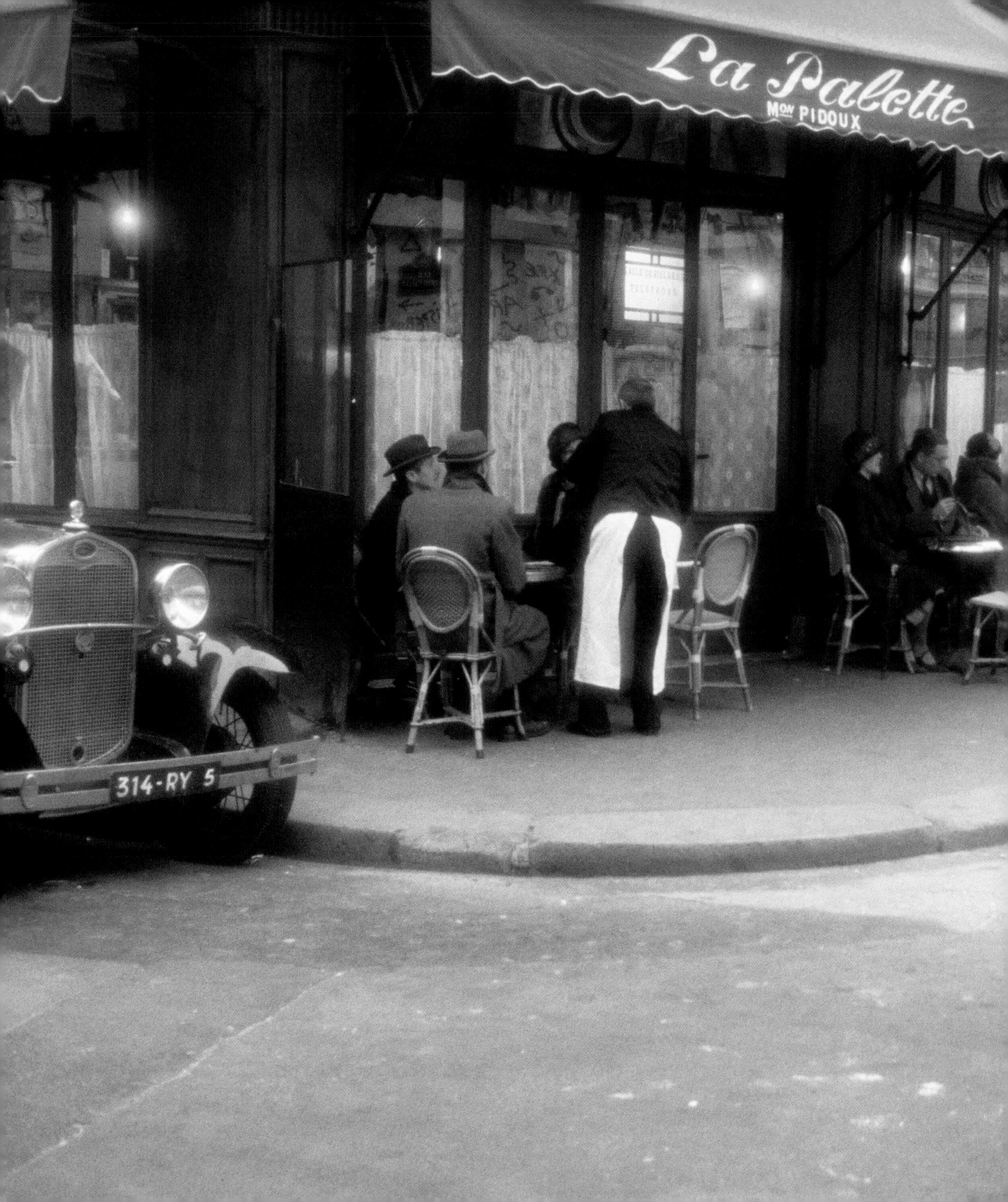

La Palette
Mon PIDOUX
314-RY 5

La Palette once more, in its 1923 incarnation, in a scene from *Quartet*. The strolling gentleman is actor Pierre Clementi.

ended the evening by sitting around the fire, talking over everything that had happened and crossing our fingers for the continued success of the film, which was opening the next day in Paris.

We would come back to Cannes with our next film, *Heat and Dust*, and even back to the villa, but we would not film again in France for another eight years, when we would return to Paris for a week to shoot *Mr. and Mrs. Bridge*. We had spent over six months living in Paris while making *Quartet*, and I had begun to feel very much at home there. The local shopkeepers knew me by name and I was a regular at the nearby brasseries. I had learned to negotiate the streets of Paris in my car, and often drove around them as if I were at home. Above all, I had established a good relationship with the French crew and technicians, in particular the cinematographer Pierre Lhomme, and had formed a close and lasting relationship with Humbert Balsan and his family. I realized that our departure from Paris marked a beginning for Merchant Ivory rather than an end. *Quartet* had been a watershed: France was no longer just a market for our films, it was a place where we could make them.

+>-<+

When we returned to France again with *Heat and Dust*, two years had passed. There was a great deal of interest in the film and, for once, we were in the enviable position of having the best distributors coming to us. This was very different from our usual scenario, which involved pursuing any and all distributors and submitting to whatever deal we could get. The Rank organization was selling the film and the territories were going fast. The only significant territory with which we hadn't yet made a deal was North America, but I felt confident we could tie that up in Cannes, and in fact, Universal Pictures took it. The film immediately pleased audiences: it was romantic and sweeping and depicted an India no one knew much about: a princely India, both glamorous and a bit sinister.

This time we had in tow our full cast of stars, with the exception of Julie Christie, who was working. But Shashi Kapoor—always a great favorite at the festival—came with his wife, Jennifer Kendal, as well as Christopher Cazenove, Nicholas Grace, and Greta Scacchi. I also invited Humbert Balsan: We had kept in close contact with him and felt it would be much less fun without him at the villa.

Returning to the Villa de la Garoupe in Antibes felt very much like returning home. We went up to our favorite bedrooms and thrust our heads out of the upstairs windows to inhale the old familiar scents: the blooming garden on the one side, the salty Mediterranean on the other. The festival hosted a dinner at Moulin de Mougins in Antibes, a Michelin four-star restaurant considered to be one of the finest in France. Converted from a sixteenth-century olive press, the rustic exterior blends so well with the pastoral landscape that the smart, stylish interior comes as a surprise. Only the rows of expensive cars, and the valets driving them off or bringing them back to their well-fed owners, give it away as a restaurant. What sets the Moulin apart from most other haute cuisine establishments in the area is the influence of local produce on the menu. We dined on lobster fricasseed in a Sauternes and pink-pepper cream sauce, noisette of lamb with aubergine cake in a thyme-flavored sauce, and finished the meal with anise ice cream. These combinations are unusual because the strict principles and refinement of haute cuisine do not normally admit the earthy elements of the Provençal table. However, at the Moulin, the two polarities meet with sensational results.

The following year we returned to Cannes with *The Bostonians*, which was not in the main competition but appeared as part of the Directors Fortnight. Our stars, Vanessa Redgrave and Christopher Reeve, had a heavy schedule of press conferences and interviews so they stayed in the town. But the rest of us, together with the young actress Madeleine Potter and her brother Paul, went back to our old headquarters, the Villa de la Garoupe.

By this time the French had begun to regard Merchant Ivory as part of their own cinema establishment, for we had now made a film in France, and we were treated with an almost familial courtesy. We were invited to all the official receptions and functions, as well as to private dinners that were hosted by the festival. And we paid our first visit to Colombe d'Or in St. Paul de Vence. This is one of the most celebrated restaurants in the world, largely through the legend—true or not—that Picasso, Miró, Dufy, Klee, and many other artists who ate there paid their bills in donated canvases. Certainly there is no other restaurant in France that can offer original Seurat, Braque, and Derain as diversion while dining. However, if the Colombe d'Or were famous only for its remarkable collection of art, it would be little more than a novelty. But the kitchen here is a serious one, and though nothing can upstage the paintings and drawings that cover the walls, the cuisine is every bit as accomplished.

St. Paul de Vence is a picturesque village high in the hills above the coast, affording a landscape and quality of light that would inevitably attract artists. Indeed, the drive from Cannes is part of the experience of dining at Colombe d'Or. At the massive wooden doors leading onto the large terrace of the restaurant a difficult decision must be made. Do you dine outside on the terrace, gazing across a breathtaking landscape of undulating hills and valleys scented with pine and oleander, or do you dine inside amidst the breathtaking art? Then there is the menu. Will it be soup of seasonal vegetables, or foie gras? Poached sea bass with mousseline sauce, or beef with Dauphinois potatoes? For me, though, there is never any question about dessert—it always has to be the memorable *soufflé flambé au Grand Marnier*.

Vineyards below the hilltop town of Ménerbes in the south of France, where several sequences of *Surviving Picasso* were shot in 1995.

Most of the time, however, we would dine at simple neighborhood bistros near Antibes. The glory of French cuisine is that, no matter on which gastronomic level you dine, you are unlikely to be disappointed. The only time I have eaten badly in France was during the dark days when nouvelle cuisine ruled the earth. I have never known anything quite so pretentious as those huge plates with dribbled designs around the edge, the disproportionately tiny morsel of food like a dot in the center. Taste was secondary to presentation: art on a plate was the object of this exercise. Fortunately, nouvelle cuisine went the way of all bad fashion—to the style graveyard. No, let me say instead that it was absorbed somehow into haute cuisine, which took what it wanted. It has left its mark—perhaps especially in desserts, where there is much dribbling still.

As a devoted fish lover, one of my greatest pleasures was to visit the small seafood restaurants right on the water for a large dish of bouillabaisse, the satisfying and flavorful stew of assorted white fish served with a rouille, a fiery red-pepper sauce. This dish originated in Marseilles, created by the local fishermen, who would build a fire of driftwood on the beach and cook in an enormous pot all the fish they had not sold that day. Every cook creates his or her own version of this splendid stew, but they all agree that bouillabaisse can only be made well on the Provençal coast. The *Provençaux* say that if the fish cannot leap straight out of the sea and into the pot, then it's too far from the source to be an authentic bouillabaisse—it's just fish stew.

We also did a great deal of dining and entertaining at home, of course. The arrival of the Merchant Ivory caravan in Cannes always raised certain expectations of us—and not just for our rather offbeat films. We had established a reputation for giving some of the best parties and most interesting dinners, and I knew that if I didn't maintain what by now had become a tradition—even if it were only a tradition for *us*—people would be very disappointed. Fortunately, the Villa de la Garoupe came with a cook—always the same gracious and gifted lady—and over the years we had developed a tremendous rapport. One of her specialties was *gigot d'agneau*—roast leg of lamb. I had often eaten this in restaurants and at peoples' homes and wondered how the French achieved the ideal state of moist pink flesh and dark crispy crust. The secret, I learned from our cook, is to turn the oven into a furnace before putting the meat in. Then, place the meat in the oven at the highest setting and blast it with heat for a few

63

minutes, depending on the size of the bone, before reducing the temperature and cooking it slowly. This method sears the meat and keeps it moist. The intensity of the flavor comes from piercing the skin around the bone before cooking and inserting slivers of garlic directly into the flesh: These disintegrate while the meat is cooking, imparting to it a wonderful flavor. Another of our cook's specialties was coq au vin, which also happened to be Shashi Kapoor's favorite dish, and whenever she was cooking it Shashi would warn her not to let me anywhere near it—he wanted the proper French version, not one that had been doctored by me.

→>-<←

In 1989 we were back in France with our film *Mr. and Mrs. Bridge.* Although it is actually set in Kansas City, the film has a short sequence in Paris on the eve of World War II, when the Bridges take their "second honeymoon" to Europe.

Paul Newman and Joanne Woodward agreed to star in *Mr. and Mrs. Bridge;* in fact, Joanne had initiated the project, which originally had been planned for television. Despite the huge success we had had with *A Room with a View,* including eight Oscar nominations and three wins, and the substantial success we had had with *Maurice,* we had not given up making, or trying to make, good low-budget movies. *Mr. and Mrs. Bridge* was to be such a film, but we suddenly found ourselves thrown into a new world of Concorde Air tickets and hotel suites at the Ritz in Paris. Irving Axelrod, the Newmans's powerful lawyer, was the man I had to convince of the reality of our meager budget, so I took him to lunch at the Russian Tea Room, a popular New York haunt of powerful agents.

For years Jim and I had flown standby to save money, and the cost of these Concorde tickets seemed like a monumental extravagance. How could we manage to send our stars to Paris in such style? A friend of mine knew a travel agent who promised to get us Concorde tickets at a very considerable discount so, naturally, I decided to buy the tickets from her. However, just before Paul and Joanne were due to leave for Paris, we discovered the tickets were stolen ones, distributed by some mafiosi who had obtained them from a travel agent in Beverly Hills, who had suddenly gone out of business.

This unfortunate fact was discovered in the most unpleasant way by Jim who, taking the Concorde to Paris one day before the Newmans, was interrogated

Mr. and Mrs. Bridge (Paul Newman and Joanne Woodward) sightseeing in Paris, where they felt—and were sometimes made to feel—they had come from another planet.

by detectives in the Concorde VIP lounge at Kennedy Airport as he was about to board. Air France allowed him to go for some reason—perhaps they took pity on him, or perhaps they thought it would look bad if someone so well known and, by now, so admired in France were kicked off the flight. He kept his cool, thank God, and managed to call me before he left to warn me about the bogus tickets. What if the Newmans were to present theirs the next night? What would they think? What would Irving Axelrod think—or do? So, I bought some brand-new Concorde tickets and tried to get my money back for the bogus ones. But, despite the rather tepid interest of the FBI, I never did. The friend of the friend would not answer her telephone, and we received threatening calls from New Jersey on her behalf telling us to lay off.

However, stolen plane tickets were not our only problem. A few days before we were due to start work we were told that Jacques Chirac, then mayor of Paris, had refused us permission to shoot in the city streets. We were completely astonished by this news, especially as Jacques Lang, the Minister of Culture, had hosted a small reception for us at the Palais Royal to celebrate our filming in Paris. Unknown to us, however, the American immigration services had recently refused to allow a French film crew to enter the United States to make a movie, thereby causing diplomatic problems with the French. As the French have always operated a liberal open-door policy toward foreign filmmakers in their country, they were offended by the American nonreciprocation. Their refusal to grant us permission to shoot on any Paris street was in retaliation to this. We called Jack Valenti, the president of the American Motion Picture Producers Association, to see if he could take some action on behalf of the French filmmakers. I also went to see Jacques Lang, who was very sympathetic, but said his hands were tied because of the intransigent attitude of the Americans.

It seemed as though this matter would not be resolved quickly, and with only eight days to film our sequences in Paris we had no time to lose. Humbert Balsan found that a French film was soon to begin shooting near the Pont Neuf, which was also one of our locations. So, he went to the *Préfecture de police*, who must give their official stamp before shooting can commence at any particular site, and, allowing it to seem—how exactly to say this?—that he was attached to the French film, asked for their endorsement, and obtained it. We were now officially sanctioned to shoot someone else's film.

Under these circumstances the first day of our shooting was, naturally, fraught with tension. The shooting took place on the quai exactly opposite Notre Dame, among the *bouquinistes*—the second-hand booksellers—whose wares are displayed in green tin boxes on the parapets overlooking the Seine. I was worried that Paul and Joanne would attract a crowd, that the crowd might draw the attention of the police, that the police might then unmask our subterfuge, and that we would all end up in jail. None of these things happened. Fortunately, the following day we heard that the American immigration authorities had relented: the French director and his technicians were being allowed to get on with their work in the United States, and we could now—legitimately—get on with ours.

Mrs. and Mr. Bridge and Notre Dame.

La Palette, now in its 1940s incarnation, on the day World War II began in a scene from *Mr. and Mrs. Bridge*.

Much had changed in Paris during the nine years since we had shot *Quartet;* but there had been no significant increase in the demand for Indian flower garlands, and again I had to construct one myself to drape over the camera on the first day of shooting. However, the San Regis hotel had changed: It had been restored and luxuriously upgraded with its rates jacked up accordingly. Happily for us, Madame Balsan, Humbert's mother, very kindly put some of us up in an apartment once again. So, I moved in with Mikki Ansin, our stills photographer, and Carol Ramsey, the costume designer, who were also staying there.

The advantage of staying at the apartment, besides the substantial financial consideration, was that I could cook for my friends. One of the first people I invited to dinner was our banker from the Bank de la Cité where we had established an account for the film. She brought as her date Jean-Pierre Leaud, one of France's leading actors, who had played François Truffaut's alter ego in many of that director's films. Fortunately, I had prepared an impressive dinner: *rouget* with capers, tandoori chicken, cauliflower and potatoes with cumin seeds, saffron rice, dal, and salad.

I anticipated that Monsieur Leaud might entertain us with stories about Truffaut and his work, but he didn't utter a single word all evening. I knew he spoke very little English so I made a tremendous effort to communicate in my fractured French, with Humbert helpfully plastering over the cracks, but Leaud remained silent throughout the entire meal. Later we learned this is normal for him, even when he is among the French: His shyness incapacitates him at social gatherings, but his taciturnity vanishes the moment he begins to act. By the end of the meal, Leaud did manage a shy smile, and we felt we had achieved some kind of breakthrough. I could see that he enjoyed my food, so perhaps we communicated that way.

Another of our locations for *Mr. and Mrs. Bridge* was La Palette, a sidewalk café on the corner of rue Jacques Callot and rue de Seine that we had also used for *Quartet*. One of the reasons it was such a useful location is that it is one of the few Parisian cafes that has not been modernized, either inside or out, and thus still retains the appearance it must have had for decades. In *Quartet*, it is where Marya Zelli is introduced to a pornographer, played by Pierre Clementi. In *Mr. and Mrs. Bridge*, La Palette is where Mr. Bridge has arranged to meet a copyist from the Louvre, who brings a present for Mrs. Bridge. While they are discussing their business, World War II breaks out and the news of Poland's invasion is heard over the café radio. As I move about my current neighborhood, shopping or on my way out to eat, I pass by La Palette almost every day. It is still a great place to quickly eat a steak *frites*, and it still resists modernization in the way of lighting, new awnings, or glass partitions over the sidewalk in winter.

On our last night in Paris I took Paul, Joanne, Jim, and Humbert to dinner at the Closerie de Lilas on the boulevard Montparnasse. I had not been there since the time of *Shakespeare Wallah*, when we were treated to lunch by our cagey distributor and financier. This old restaurant has, for more than a hundred years, attracted the most illustrious names in the literary, artistic, and political worlds of Paris. Many of the tables are inscribed with the names of their one-time occupants such as Picasso, Appollinaire, Cocteau, Dalí, and Modigliani. Even Lenin and Trotsky are said to have been regulars here. Ernest Hemingway supposedly wrote *The Sun Also Rises* while he sat on the tree-fringed terrace. However, his name is inscribed not on a table but, perhaps more appropriately, on the bar.

After eight days in Paris we moved to Kansas City to shoot the bulk of *Mr. and Mrs. Bridge*, and were absolutely astonished to discover that it was also the location of the French film that had had immigration problems. So, we became friendly with the French crew, and one Sunday challenged them to a baseball

Two baseball teams, one French, the other American, in Kansas City during filming of Mr. and Mrs. Bridge in 1989. The nominal captains were the French director Eli Chauraqui and James Ivory.

game. They accepted, which was sporting of them because baseball is virtually unknown in France and they were not familiar with the game. However, they almost beat us—one point more and the two teams would have tied. We had a lot of athletic women on our team and we credit them with most of our home runs. The French sang "La Marseillaise" after every one of their home runs. Afterward we had a real Kansas City barbecue with three kinds of meat: beef, pork, and chicken, with Kansas City barbecue sauce and all the baked beans, potato salad, and cornbread we could eat. Then both teams posed for a group photo.

→>-<-

In 1992 we finally went to Cannes with a film that was both an established box-office hit and a critical triumph. We were presenting *Howards End*, which had opened in America a few weeks earlier. It would become our most successful film to date, and would be nominated for nine Academy Awards: Emma Thompson would receive the Oscar for best actress and Ruth Jhabvala would receive a second Oscar for her screenplay, proving what Merchant Ivory had been arguing with film financiers for so many years—that our kind of independent and idiosyncratic filmmaking did not preclude commercial success. But,

in addition to having one of the most eagerly awaited films of the festival, Merchant Ivory had another cause for celebration: It had been thirty years to the very month since Jim and I formed our partnership.

Unfortunately, it was no longer possible for us to rent the Villa La Garoupe in Antibes, a house and a place so full of enjoyable memories for us. The property had been sold, and Humbert warned us not even to drive past it, so complete (and devastating to memories) had been the renovation. Instead, we rented the Château de Garibondy in the hills of Le Cannet high above the old port of Cannes. This was a real fairy-tale château—white, romantically turreted, and, in a minor way, historic. Queen Victoria had visited the château and planted the umbrella pine that now towered majestically over the three stories of the building. On one of the terraces that overlooked the flower-filled garden with its banks of rose bushes in brilliant bloom, was a fountain whose waters, according to legend, contained magical youth-preserving properties. A fountain of youth is the hope of all who sojourn in the south of France, most especially movie-makers, I think.

The château was large and I made sure it was full. In addition to Helena Bonham Carter, James Wilby, Sam West, and Adrian Ross Magenty, all of whom appeared in *Howards End*, I brought along my executive producer Paul Bradley, and friends such as Humbert, Shashi Kapoor, and Richard Robbins, who had composed the score for the film and who was at Cannes for the first time—even though he had scored every film we had presented in the festival since *The Europeans*. Jim had also invited friends, and various other guests, crew members, and colleagues would come and go over the fortnight.

There was one drawback to the château: In the entire huge building, there was only one telephone and it was situated on the ground floor in a sort of "cabin." At night the queue for this telephone, with people calling the United States where everyone was still at work, was something to see—and dread. Once we had all made it to bed and all the lights had been turned out, well after midnight, the phone would still continue to ring. Now it was people waking up in India who were calling to talk to me or to Shashi. And as the day approached when our film would be shown, there were more and more callers, and of course more calls to be made.

The stars of *Howards End*—Anthony Hopkins, Vanessa Redgrave, Emma

Thompson, and Helena Bonham Carter—were all working and therefore
unable to be with us during the festival. However, as our screening was on a
Sunday, they all agreed to come to Cannes for the occasion to share our special
day. Stars mean a lot to festivals because they add glamour to the event and
ensure publicity for the film—often one of a festival's conditions for accepting a
film is the promise that the stars will attend. I chartered a private jet to bring
Vanessa, Helena, and Emma from London, and another jet to bring Anthony
from Berlin where he was shooting a film. The production company in Berlin
had been reluctant to let Tony leave for even a day—perhaps they thought he
would be kept from returning by this unreliable mix of French festival organizers and ourselves—frivolous, unserious people all.

Everything had been arranged so that all four actors would arrive in time
for the morning press conference. But then we heard that the plane bringing
Vanessa, Helena, and Emma was delayed, and then we lost Tony somewhere
between his hotel in Berlin and the airport in Berlin. Frantic calls were coming
and going between France, Germany, and England, and we were also trying to
deal with an increasingly anxious festival director, Giles Jacob, who had been

Three English beauties from the
film *Howards End*: The Schlegel
sisters with Leonard Bast in the
south of France (left to right: Helena
Bonham Carter, Emma Thompson,
and Sam West).

promised at least three stars. We sympathize with the fretting festival director, anxiously standing at the top of the festival palace stairs and looking at his watch. He knows the fashionably dressed audience inside will not be pleased if he disappoints them and the promised quota of stars does not turn up. He will be blamed for a dull gala—for the film being presented is not the only thing the people in the audience have come to see.

Eventually we discovered that Tony had been taken to the airport at six in the morning where he had waited patiently for four hours for the private jet to arrive. The private jet had also been waiting for four hours; unfortunately, at a different airport. As soon as I heard what had happened I called Tony, who had returned to his hotel, and tried to persuade him to go to the other airport where our plane was still waiting for him. But Tony was so exasperated by then that he decided not to come at all. Everybody was sure that the German production company in Berlin had deliberately sent Tony to the wrong airport, but there was nothing to be done.

The plane from London was due to arrive forty minutes after our press conference commenced. I went to the airport to meet Vanessa, Helena, and Emma, while Jim and the others at the château went on ahead to the press conference. Two limousines, with a police escort, sped us from the airport to the Palais, and Vanessa, Helena, Emma, and I made our entrance to yells from the crowd of journalists and photographers, and to audible sighs of relief from the festival authorities. For, if the audiences at a Cannes gala like celebrities—like meeting them or just being in the same room with them for a few hours—journalists are no different. They may direct their questions to the directors out of professional necessity, but those they direct to the stars give them more pleasure, no matter what the answers may be.

After the press conference, we had a lunch at the château for all the journalists and critics. Tables had been set up in the garden, white-coated waiters greeted the guests with iced champagne, and cooks were busily preparing foie gras and pheasant in the kitchen. A central table on the terrace held a huge celebratory cake decorated with the legend "M I P 30 YEARS." Around it were a number of smaller cakes—strawberry, chocolate, caramel, cream—each one a triumph of the *pâtissiere*'s art. Despite the chaos of the morning I had managed to find time to prepare a large pot of dal, because a meal without dal just isn't a proper meal. I had no idea where it fit into the French menu prepared by the caterers, but it was a success with the guests, who enjoyed the occasion so much that at six o'clock in the afternoon they were still sitting at the tables, under Queen Victoria's tree, enjoying their coffee and liqueurs. At a festival, the press lunch is usually eaten quickly as the journalists all have films to see and appointments to keep—when the dessert and coffee appear, you know that they will soon be off. There is always something of an exodus as people go in search of the next—or better—event, but on that day we all left pretty much together in order to make it to the Palais on time for our screening.

Eight cars, official pennants flying, raced us down the hill to Cannes. But, as soon as we reached the Croisette our cavalcade came to a sudden halt: The whole of the Croisette was full of people pressing up against our windows trying to see who was inside. I had never seen anything like it before. Slowly we inched our way to the Palais, and as we emerged from the cars, dusk suddenly became daylight as a thousand flashbulbs exploded around us. The front of the new Palais at Cannes is a bit like a high Aztec temple, with very steep steps covered in a blood-red carpet. You mount the steps slowly as the photographers take pictures and the crowd far below yells. At the top stands the festival director, bowing and gesturing in welcome, flanked by guardians who keep out the unticketed and the badly dressed.

As we entered the auditorium the whole audience rose in expectation and we were greeted with another burst of applause. The lights went down and the film began. Halfway through the opening credits, during the image of Vanessa walking in her garden at Howards End, the reel spluttered and stopped. We waited a moment. Nothing happened. The lights went up again and we made appropriate faces and gestures of surprise. I sent someone to find out what was going on. They returned a few moments later to report that the projector had malfunctioned. The film began again. And again, in almost the very same place, the reel stopped. Humbert and I went into the projection booth to see what was happening.

Meanwhile, the audience was waiting, and the impatient buzz was growing louder. We were told the break in the reel would take a while to repair, and, standing in the projection box like a captain on the bridge, I felt as if I were on the sinking *Lusitania*. I could hear the murmurs of the audience getting louder; then, suddenly, they diminished until there was silence. Had they left? I looked out of the projection booth and saw that Vanessa, unprompted, had stood up and was addressing the audience in French. She, the most English of English goddesses, was taming the French audience. She graciously apologized for the delay, explaining there was a mechanical problem that was being corrected, and she begged everyone's indulgence and patience. If ever proof were needed of just how brilliant an actress Vanessa is, this occasion provided it. She was quite capable of saying her piece perfectly in rapid idiomatic French; but, instead, her delivery was a little halting and unsure, as if she were making an effort—a charming one at that—to communicate with the audience in their own ever-so-difficult language. She won them over completely. By the time the applause for Vanessa's speech had died down, the broken film was finally spliced together, and at the end of the screening we received a ten-minute standing ovation—one that I'm sure was prompted by good sportsmanship. Mrs. Wilcox, the spiritual center of *Howards End*, had stepped down from the screen to make things right.

Apart from the vexing habit of the younger element of our party to roll home in the early hours without their cab fares or front door keys, this was the most relaxed festival fortnight I had ever known. Without the pressure of chasing financiers and distributors, I could enjoy the leisurely lunch parties and dinners at the château, swim in the pool, go to films, shop at the market—or visit restaurants that were new to me.

One day Humbert took us all to Eden Roc in Antibes, and we lunched outside on the terrace, from which the only view is water. With a swimming pool on one side and the shimmering blue waters of the Mediterranean on the other, it was almost like being on a ship. Humbert ordered a huge sea bass for us and, like the pheasant at Satyajit Ray's party, the grilled bass with its spectacular garnish of sculpted vegetables was brought out on a platter and presented to us before being taken away to be served. To accompany this magnificent fish we drank a Domaines Ott, Côtes de Provence, a local wine that is crisp, aromatic, and delicious. I don't normally make a habit of remembering wines because, although I enjoy a fine bottle and know how to appreciate a great bottle, I am not a connoisseur. However, this wine was quite a find as Provence is not generally known for its wines, even though the Greeks, who introduced viticulture to France, planted the first vines here in the south of France.

On our last Sunday we visited the Fondation Maeght to see their collection of modern sculpture and painting, and then lunched at Le Diamant Rose, a very good restaurant in a converted Provençal villa in the tiny hilltop hamlet of Le Colle sur Loup. Again, we celebrated the success of *Howards End* with a memorable lunch: This time we had lamb on layers of aubergine in a richly caramelized sauce, and a variety of desserts, such as nougat ice cream, chocolate mousse cake, strawberries and cream, and other confections so exquisite that each plate was passed round for everyone to taste. The following night at the award ceremony Jim was presented with a special festival prize for the body of his work, awarded to him as a consolation prize for not having won anything else for *Howards End*. The prize, a rolled-up scroll with nothing yet printed on it, was bestowed in commemoration of the festival's forty-fifth year. It was a fitting end to a fabulous fortnight.

➜➤◄✦

In 1993 Jim and I were in Paris again for the opening of *The Remains of the Day*. Although the film was highly successful in America and England, we were worried that the French might not respond to it in the same way. After the opening, we were taken to dinner by the French executives of Columbia Pictures in Paris, and around midnight we went back to their offices to see what the opening-day admissions had been. We watched the name of each French city, with its corresponding admission figures, come up on a large computer screen, and as the results came in, the distributors began to clap with excitement. Soon, a bottle of champagne was opened. We have been through many of these first nights in various parts of the world, but seldom have we seen such big smiles on the faces of our distributors.

While we were in Paris, we were invited to dinner by Liliane de Rothschild at her splendid house. One reason for this treat was that Liliane's sister, whose nickname was "Bubbles," was Helena Bonham Carter's grandmother. But there was another reason: Liliane de Rothschild has compiled a choice collection of objects that belonged to Louis XVI and Marie Antoinette, such as works of art, autographed letters, and so forth. She knew from Helena that we were planning to make a film about the years Thomas Jefferson spent as the American ambassador to France, from 1784 to 1789. She knew that the film would touch on the life of the ancien régime and she thought she might be able to help us with that. In her dining room that night hung a portrait of Madame du Barry, Louis XV's last mistress who, legend has it, owned the accursed Hope diamond. Four white-gloved waiters attended us, and our host, the baron, told funny stories that helped us relax. The sumptuous dinner, served on a dinner service that had belonged to Madame du Barry, began with a superb pâte de foie gras on a bed of *frisée*, followed by beef Richelieu—a joint of roasted fillet garnished with braised lettuce, tomatoes, tiny roasted potatoes, and mushroom caps filled with a mushroom purée. Dessert was a refreshing sorbet with fresh berries. Naturally, the wines were vintage Mouton Rothschild.

After dinner, Madame de Rothschild showed us some of her treasures, such as a box of velvet purses that were used at the French court by members of the royal family and nobility when they were gambling. The box contained Marie Antoinette's purse as well: a velvet pouch embroidered with fleurs-de-lys that opened and shut with a cord. We learned from one of the other guests that Louis XVI spoke English, the only French king who did, and that he read the British newspapers. He knew English well enough to translate Shakespeare's *Richard III* into French, and Liliane de Rothschild showed us a copy of this little book. Because of what we learned that night, we wrote an exchange in English between the king and Jefferson, who is being presented at court: "Have you found a good house yet? It's very important to have a good house in Paris," the king asks the ambassador.

Our idea for *Jefferson in Paris* had originated in the early 1980s. Research for the film had originally been underwritten by Avance sur Recettes, a French government film development plan, which gave us one million francs. The French have a high regard for Jefferson and his ideals, which mirrored those of their own politician, Lafayette. Later, Tri-Star commissioned Ruth Jhabvala's screenplay and later still Disney decided to finance the picture, putting up the bulk of the fourteen-million-dollar budget because of Jeffrey Katzenburg's enthusiasm for the project and for working with us.

Nick Nolte was cast as Jefferson, Greta Scacchi as his beloved friend Maria Cosway, Simon Callow as Cosway's husband, Gwyneth Paltrow as Jefferson's daughter Patsy, and Thandie Newton as the slave Sally Hemings, whom Jefferson brought to Paris. The production would be on an epic scale: We intended to shoot court scenes at Versailles; re-create the Cirque at the Palais Royal; build

Opposite, above: Marie Antoinette (Charlotte de Turckheim) stops to speak to Thomas Jefferson and his daughter Patsy (Nick Nolte and Gwyneth Paltrow) at Versailles, in a scene from *Jefferson in Paris.*

Opposite, below: Thomas Jefferson presents his credentials as ambassador to Louis XVI. Each time, and there were many, the king was mentioned in Jefferson's speech, protocol at Versailles demanded that everyone present—including the king—remove his hat.

Above: Jefferson in Paris extras
waiting in line in one of the
Versailles galleries to have their
makeup and hair done.

Left: The Hall of Mirrors at Versailles
as the royal family returns from
Sunday Mass.

the set of an opera house in order to stage a late Baroque opera; launch the Montgolfier brothers' hot-air balloon and, of course, show the beginnings of the French Revolution.

We soon realized that re-creating the Paris of the twenties for *Quartet* had been easy compared to the task of re-creating the Paris of two hundred years ago. Paris appears deceptively ancient until it is exposed to the penetrating eye of the camera, and once again we relied on the skill of cinematographer Pierre Lhomme. We also brought in the knowledgeable French art historian Hervé Gransart as a location consultant, who was invaluable in suggesting little-known locations that would approximate those Jefferson had known, or real ones that still existed such as the marvelous folly known as the Désert de Retz outside Paris to which Jefferson often retreated. Wherever possible, of course, we tried to use such existing authentic locations. The most important of these was the palace of Versailles, the seat of the French monarchy and a place Jefferson visited frequently. However, permission to shoot at Versailles was long in coming, and the prospect of making the film without the Hall of Mirrors or the Queen's staircase—up which diplomats traditionally mounted for their presentation of credentials—without, in short, the overwhelming majesty of the Palace and all it represented, was simply unthinkable. We persisted in badgering the authorities until they finally agreed to allow us access to the newly refurbished interior. The severe limitations they imposed on us were gradually lifted one by one. We even devised a way of protecting the parquet and marble floors by putting the feet of our light stands into halved tennis balls so that no scratch, no mark, would be left anywhere.

There was just one hurdle left to overcome—shooting the hot-air balloon from the roof of the palace. "Absolutely not," I was told by the authorities, "Access to the roof is strictly prohibited. You may damage the lead tiles on it." Faced with such an adamant refusal, there was only one thing to do. We invited the custodian of Versailles—a woman who was most charming, but fiercely opposed to any roof shooting—to lunch on the set. She brought her daughter with her, and by one of those lucky strokes of fate, the daughter was very interested in Indian philosophy and mysticism. Over lunch I discussed those topics with her and invited her to India. By the time we got to coffee I began to broach the subject of the roof to her mother again, expressing my regret at the prohibition since it was such a glorious afternoon that the balloon scene shot from the van-

Above: Thomas Jefferson and Maria Cosway (Greta Scacchi) at the Désert de Retz, a folly of avante-garde architectural oddities outside Paris that Jefferson loved to visit. Floorplans of the circular house, constructed with many elliptical spaces inside a truncated Doric column, provided Jefferson with architectural ideas for buildings he was planning in Virginia. The plan of the Rotunda at the University of Virginia was partly based on the column house at Désert de Retz.

Opposite, above: During the shooting of *Jefferson in Paris* at Versailles: What many people imagine the lunch break on a Merchant Ivory film set to be like, except for the white plastic chairs, *bien sûr.*

Opposite, below: The audience at the opera, *Dardanus:* in the box on the left sits the Indian delegation, sent to France by Tipu Sultan to ask for French help against the British; in the box on the right sit the Cosways with Lafayette. The set was built entirely in a studio, for there are no longer any 18th-century opera houses left in Paris.

tage of the roof would have really looked spectacular. Put like this, and following a conversation about spiritualism, what could the custodian do but give way? She said if it were absolutely essential she would allow us to put a *few* people on the roof. The cast, the extras, the camera team, and a couple of assistants would amount to twenty people at least. In filmmaking terms, twenty *is* a very small number for a crew, cast, and extras, but if you are the custodian of an historic château, it seems like a lot of weight to have in one spot. We explained how we could separate this weight—the crew would be at a distance from the royal family and courtiers, who would move along as the balloon passed. Jim drew a sketch. Finally she relented and we rushed to make arrangements before sunset for what would turn out to be one of the most beautiful shots in the film—perhaps *the* most beautiful of all.

The lunch, prepared by our caterer, had been unusually good that day. Catering up to three meals a day for hundreds of people is one of the greatest responsibilities on a film set, and it is a matter every producer must take very seriously. On *Jefferson* I not only had the problem of feeding vast numbers, but the additional problem of most of those numbers being French: If they were served anything less than a superbly prepared and presented three-course meal, I would have a real revolution on my hands.

With most films, a catering truck dispenses lunch to long lines of patient actors and crew. I have always tried to provide something better than that, but in France I knew I would have to do something better still. Napoleon's aphorism that an army marches on its stomach could just as well apply to a film unit. Napoleon always took his chefs when he went into battle, and many classic French dishes were invented on the battlefield. The cooking for our troops was the responsibility of Alex Grousset, a brilliant young chef who had worked at Baumann in Paris, and he surpassed even my highest hopes. Every morning there was coffee and fresh croissants for the earliest arrivals, as well as ham and eggs for the English crew members. By midmorning, tables were piled with bread, cheese, cold meats, pâtès, and fruit. At lunchtime, and dinner if we were working late, Alex produced delicious and imaginative two-course meals followed by salad and dessert, served on properly laid tables by efficient waiters. And, because wine is integral to a French meal, there were always appropriate wines.

Alex managed to repeat this feat day after day, whether we were shooting in a château where he had access to a kitchen, or in the middle of the woods with no facilities whatsoever. Even when he had to cook for hundreds of extras, his standards never dropped. Film extras, usually the poor relations on a set, are often left to fend for themselves, but at Versailles, the caterers laid protective plastic over the floor of one of the vast chambers and then carefully filled it with tables. For the actors and the principle members of the unit, tables were laid outside under canvas awnings. Astonishingly, there was even a choice of menu.

In addition to his duties on the film, Alex was always ready to assist when I cooked for my on-set parties, and we cooked together that year for Jim's birthday. Alex never turned a hair at what he may have considered my unconventional antics in the kitchen. He told me that I was, in fact, simply doing what the French have always done—taking the best culinary ideas from other cultures and making them their own. La Varenne, the great chef of Louis XIV, the Sun King, took classic roast beef from England as the basis for a number of his dishes. When Catherine de Medici married Henry II of France in 1533, she brought her chefs from Florence with her, along with their specialties from the Italian

A scene from *Jefferson in Paris* depicting the type of bread riots that were a prelude to the French Revolution. Delicious French bread is well worth rioting for.

court. It was the Italians who first brought cooking as we know it to France, and the French who developed it into the art it is today.

Louis XVI, the doomed king of our film, but a great gourmand, is said to have sent out fleets of ships to bring new and unfamiliar ingredients for his dinner table from exotic lands. In *Jefferson in Paris*, we showed a tableau of the king at table: It was the custom, and a great honor, for members of the court to stand and watch the king eat, and on certain holidays the public was permitted to view the king as he dined, moving past him in a long line, as we depict in our scene.

Whenever we were shooting at a location in an area that was new to me I would be torn between sampling more of Alex's delightful cooking on the set and investigating the local restaurants. In Versailles I became a frequent visitor to the Brasserie du Théâtre, a classic brasserie gleaming with polished brass that produced a truly memorable cassoulet, the stew of duck, sausage, and beans that is one of the great dishes of *cuisine paysanne*. Cassoulet originated in Languedoc, and there is a rivalry between the towns of Toulouse, Carcassonne, Castelnaudry, and even between towns in the neighboring regions of Perigord and Gascony, over where the dish was invented and who produces the correct version. The French novelist Anatole France came out in favor of Castelnaudry's claim, describing it as the "godfather" of all cassoulets. To understand how a pot of stew can provoke such passions, one obviously needs to sample the dish in all the towns that claim it as their own—perhaps someday I will be able to do that.

→>-<←

Ruth's visits to the set are so rare that when she came to Paris with her husband, Cyrus, during the shooting of *Jefferson* I took them, along with Jim and some of the actors in the film, to lunch at Le Grand Vefour. We had been shooting that day in the North Gallery of the Palais Royal, only a few steps away from the restaurant, where I had never been. Its location opposite the gardens of the Palais Royal, and its authentic eighteenth-century painted, wood-paneled, and mirrored interior, are the perfect setting for a restaurant considered to be one of the beacons of French gastronomy. For nearly two hundred years, French celebrities from Napoleon to André Malraux, Victor Hugo, Cocteau, and Colette have come here to dine, and today it still attracts artists, writers, politicians, and movie stars. We were not let down that day: I can still recall the subtlety of the asparagus-and-

Above: The wicker gondola of the Montgolfier balloon aloft over the Versailles gardens with its passengers —a sheep, a duck, and a rooster—all of whom returned safely to earth.

Opposite: The first ascent of a hot-air balloon in 1783 attracted a crowd of 100,000 curious people. The royal family, observing the scene from the roof of the château, were overcome by the foul odors of the burning gases used to lift the balloon and had to retreat from the historic spectacle.

The entrance to Le Grand Vefour restaurant in
the Palais Royal. At right, the interior of Le Grand
Vefour, the most beautiful old restaurant in Paris.

truffle bouillon and the intensity of the roast pigeon. The richness of Le Grand Vefour—the setting itself, the exquisite food, and the hushed service—is not something one should experience every day; neither one's wallet nor one's digestion would allow that. But it is certainly, among Parisian restaurants, the place to celebrate a grand occasion.

It was during the shooting at Versailles that the enormity of our operation really hit me. The endless broad corridors of the palace became makeshift dressing rooms packed with bodies being fit into military uniforms and elaborate court dress. Hatboxes were piled high to the frescoed ceilings, and rows of boots and shoes snaked along the corridors. These regal spaces echoed with the imperative and urgent demands of an army of ancillary personnel—hairdressers, makeup artists, wardrobe assistants, runners, and more assistants. Outside, another equally populous crew was preparing to inflate and put into orbit an exact replica of the first hot-air balloon that the Montgolfier brothers brought to Versailles to demonstrate to Louis XVI. With a circumference of almost six hundred feet, it was a stretch limo of a balloon, and as it swelled up with air, it seemed to take on a life of its own, embracing and devouring everything around it. I heard someone quip, "We could turn this into a horror film, *The Blob That Ate Versailles.*" I was being visited by my worst nightmare: my own film unit operating on a Hollywood scale, in which every man and woman has to be paid, fed, and per diemed. Every powdered wig, every carefully chosen rifle, every swag and tassel on the balloon, was for me in this nightmare a symbol of potential bankruptcy. But then I would watch the rushes—the majestic procession through the Hall of Mirrors, the heart-stopping ascent of the balloon with the palace in the background and the army of courtiers following its course through the gardens—and I knew that every centime had been well spent.

For this balloon scene, the weather had to be on our side. A balloon cannot go up in a wind storm, or when there is any wind at all, for that matter, and still remain in place for the cameras below (there were three). Too much breeze and the unwieldy balloon, tethered by ropes, would blow out of the frame, or up against the palace—and we wanted it directly in front of the palace. The times of day when a balloon can best ascend are at dawn and dusk when there is less wind. So we split our day, and shot just as the sun was rising, and then again when it was setting. The winds were kind, the sun did not disappear behind

Merchant, costumed as Tipu Sultan's emissary, in an uncharacteristically patient mood while being subjected to the minutiae of correct period makeup.

the clouds, and the sequence was realized—the most complicated certainly, though perhaps the most beautiful, of all Merchant Ivory crowd scenes.

Even though Jim had a thousand bodies at his disposal for the shots, he decided he needed one more—mine. Jim wanted to introduce an emissary of Tipu Sultan, the Nawab of Mysore, to the French court, and he thought the opera scene would be an appropriate place for his appearance. These Indian diplomats were the talk of Paris when they turned up in the 1780s, looking for an ally against the British. To amuse themselves, they truly did attend the opera, where it was noted that they sat eating ices with their feet up on the edge of the box. I have, from time to time, played cameo roles or walk-ons in some of our films, and as this never takes up more than a few hours of my time, I agreed to become Tipu Sultan's emissary.

Jim gave me a good piece of business for the role. When Jefferson appears at the opera and takes his place in the adjoining box, the audience applauds him. But Tipu's ambassador, being also the talk of Paris, thinks the crowd is applauding *him*. He half-rises and begins to acknowledge this applause, until he realizes it is for the occupant of the next box, whereupon he sits down in embarrassment. Well, we have all had such moments in life and my portrayal of the chastened ambassador is not too bad. His true fate was much sadder: When he returned to India without a French promise of help, he was beheaded.

My first indication that my acquiescence had been a very serious mistake was when I had to join, at dawn, the other extras on set for costuming and elaborate makeup. I wore a long, bushy, and very irritating moustache—copied from the one in the portrait of the ambassador painted by Vigée-Lebrun—and then I was dressed in elaborate red-and-gold robes with unwieldy sleeves and a train. I was jeweled and turbaned, and though no doubt thoroughly authentic in every way, felt rather ridiculous and extremely uncomfortable. Never mind, I thought, at least it will soon be over. In the meantime I could take some pleasure in listening to William Christie and his orchestra Les Arts Florissants—bewigged and costumed like everyone else—perform Sacchini's *Dardanus* on period instruments in our specially constructed opera house.

But Baroque opera is complicated to stage: singers descending from the flies, set changes for the many ballet sequences, and arias that are beautiful, if long, to listen to. Six hours after being costumed I still hadn't been called for my scene. By then I was beginning to wonder what I had got myself into, and even began to feel some compassion for actors whose daily lot this is. Finally, after lunch, I was called to the set and put into a box with my attendants, one of whom was my nephew Nayeem Hafizka, an assistant director on the film. Nayeem began his career as an actor before following my footsteps into producing and directing, so he has had somewhat more experience acting than I have. This, however, did not prevent me from giving him advice. I explained to him that every gesture is magnified on the screen, so each expression and movement must be very subtle and controlled.

At one of the pauses in the shooting that long, long day, Simon Callow, who had a prominent part in this scene, came over to my box. Simon is an old friend who has appeared in a number of our films and who directed *The Ballad of the Sad Café* for us. "Ismail," he said sternly, "I am going to call the acting police and have you arrested. They will come and slap a ticket on you. Your performance is a disgrace and a scandal and constitutes the most unprofessional behavior. Where is your Equity card? It should be torn up." He gave me a long, disapproving stare. "Now that I've seen you like this," he continued, indicating my elaborate costume, turban, and long mustache, "I'll never be able to take you seriously as a producer again." Given that he was sporting an excessively busy wig sprigged with diamonds, and was wearing chalk-white makeup, crimson lipstick, and a beauty spot, I told him he was in no position to make judgments on others.

My outfit as Tipu Sultan's emissary appeared almost conservative compared to the vestments I had to wear at my induction into the *Commanderie du Bontemps de Medoc et des Graves*. This is a society composed of the leading vineyard proprietors in Bordeaux into which I was elected as an honorary member. This opportunity arose from a visit we made to Sylvie Cazes-Ragimbeau, a distant relative of Humbert Balsan, who had invited us to her home in Bordeaux.

I was very keen to see Bordeaux as it is the most important wine-growing region in France; the home of Rothschild, Margaux, Latour, Lafite, Petrus, and all the other historic names that represent the pinnacle of the winemaker's art. As we drove to Sylvie's mother's house for lunch, I had a slightly surreal moment as I noticed a confluence of signs pointing to well-known wineries: St. Estèphe in one direction, Pauillac in another, Pomerol to the right, St. Emilion to the left, St. Julian to the north, and Graves to the south. It was like driving through an incredibly rich wine-merchant's cellar.

Above: Merchant's table set for lunch.

Below: An ornate dessert from a rue de Buci pâtisserie.

It is no surprise that the Bordelaise have developed a highly refined cuisine to accompany these great wines, making Bordeaux one of the most important gastronomic centers of the country. The Bordelaise style is a classic of haute cuisine, and the term *à la bordelaise* indicates a cooking method which, inevitably, features a red-wine sauce. For lunch we had one of the specialties of the region: *agneau de lait de Pauillac*, milk-fed lamb from the salty marshlands of the Landes, bordering on the Atlantic coast. Reared by ewes who graze on grass impregnated with sea salt, the lamb has an intense, slightly salty flavor, and is prepared very simply with herbs, garlic, and a little wine vinegar. With this we drank a very fine Lynch-Bages, the house wine as it were, for I discovered that my hostess owned the Château Lynch-Bages, one of the great wine-producing châteaux.

We talked about Jefferson, who was a great connoisseur of wine and kept a very impressive cellar. During his tenure at the White House he and his guests consumed enormous quantities and he was strongly criticized for it. He wrote frequently on the subject of wine, observing that he had never seen a drunk Frenchman because, unlike Americans who drank whisky, the French drank wine, and he thought all Americans should follow their example. He certainly made Americans more aware of wine, and even tried to cultivate vines at his estate at Monticello, but did not have great success and concluded that wine could never be a product of the United States. He ordered cases and cases of Meursault, a white wine he adored, for Monticello. This was no doubt one of the extravagances that eventually drove him into debt. He would have been happy to imagine the enormous success and prestige of wine growers on the West Coast almost two hundred years later.

Perhaps it was the combination of my interest in cooking, my authorship of a number of cookbooks, our film about the wine connoisseur Jefferson, and my own appreciation of the fruits of Château Lynch-Bages that prompted Madame Cazes-Regimbeau to invite me into the *Commanderie*. The ceremony was to take place in June, while we were shooting *Jefferson*. As it fell on a Saturday, it was possible for me to attend, but getting to Bordeaux and back in one day from Paris was going to be difficult. I had a standing invitation from a friend who owns a helicopter company to take an aerial tour of Paris, which I traded in for a round-trip excursion to Bordeaux. The helicopter couldn't accommodate all the friends I wanted to take with me so some, including Gwyneth Paltrow, who was also going to be inducted into the *Commanderie*, took the train the previous night and stayed at the château.

The rest of us flew out on a gray, drizzly morning, the weather getting progressively worse as we neared Bordeaux. We landed in a boggy field, and as we were coming down I was astonished to see a television crew from the BBC filming our arrival. They were there to make a series about wine, and when they heard that I was coming to join in the *Fête de la Fleur* celebrations they wanted to include it in their film. Our arrival certainly made impressive footage: a movie producer arriving like a legendary film mogul in a private state-of-the-art helicopter. Who will ever pay attention to me now, I thought, when I argue about expenses and budgets, or when I try to keep down the costs of our stars, who also like private helicopters and other such conveniences.

The ceremony is held at a different château each year and this time it was to be at Château Lilian Ladouys at St. Estèphe. Our sponsor, Sylvie, led Gwyneth and me down to the vaulted cellars and onto a stage to join the other inductees. There we were robed in floor-length velvet cloaks of green and red—the colors of the vine—and handed a glass of red wine. We stood holding glasses of wine in a semicircle around a symbolic wooden bowl while the ceremony took place, and then we were pronounced members of a great family. Drummers and pipers in medieval costume escorted us from the stage to that part of the cellar where the 1993 vintage was stored—we would be the first to enjoy the privilege of tasting it.

Outside, the rain was streaming down, and we ran to the marquee for what was certainly the longest lunch I have ever known. The tables were beautifully laid with porcelain, linen napkins bound with ribbon and the wax seal of the château, and a remarkable number of wineglasses at each place setting. Sylvie explained that eight different Bordeaux wines would be served with the seven-course lunch, which had been created by Jean-Pierre Vigato of the Parisian restaurant Apicius. In addition, there was champagne to accompany the opening speeches, and cognac for the closing ones.

This feast began with an *amuse-bouche*, literally translated as a little thing to entertain the mouth, then we moved on to smoked trout, crayfish with tomato confit and basil, cod with a crust of spice, classic pigeon tart with foie gras and mushrooms; all followed by cheese, *gâteau* of chocolate, pears and ginger with vanilla ice cream, then petits fours. Between each course an ensemble of a dozen

Ismail Merchant, the new Honorary Commander des Bontemps de Medoc et des Graves, 1994.

singers entertained us with serenades to wine, in addition to other drinking songs, and dancers enacted historic scenes associated with the château. Before each course was served, waiters paraded the accompanying wines around the marquee, receiving even more applause than the performers—but that was the kind of day it was.

There was one moment of horror when one of my guests found a live worm crawling out of the cod. Jake Paltrow, Gwyneth's brother, brought this to her attention just as she was about to eat it. Naturally, this caused something of a flap among the non-French, which baffled our hostess. "You know, in France we eat *everything*," she said with Gallic insouciance.

Lunch went on until the early evening, when we accompanied Sylvie and her party back to the Château Lynch-Bages, where we drank yet more wine in a private celebration of the occasion. The rain had eased off, so we went on a much-needed walk around the vineyards of the estate, which were vast. Row upon row of carefully tended vines stretched far into the otherwise featureless horizon. We had seen the impressive sight of the entire region's vineyards from the air as we flew into Bordeaux, but only at ground level could I truly understand the scale of this industry.

As we wandered through the vineyards I took great pleasure listening to Sylvie talk so knowledgeably and with such passion on the subject of wine. It seemed impossible to me that this thin gravelly soil could support the lush vegetation, which, in turn, sustains the fat grapes that produce the voluptuous, complex red wines that rank as the finest in the world; nor did it seem possible that the region could yield up to 600 million bottles each year. Sylvie explained that it was precisely this inhospitable soil that was responsible for the character of the wine. Outside the immediate area of Bordeaux, the soil becomes more fertile and the wine, though still perfectly respectable, is lighter and less intense.

The Graves region of Bordeaux, the principal white-wine producing area, is known for the white wines of Sauternes and Barsac, which are traditionally drunk with foie gras. The greatest of these is Château d'Yquem, and it is said that it takes the grapes of an entire vine to produce a single glass of this powerful, aromatic wine—which explains its cost, and why it is sometimes referred to as "liquid gold." Sylvie told us that the long warm autumns in Graves, together with morning dew and afternoon sun, provide the ideal conditions for the grapes to be infected with "noble rot," which is what gives this wine its unique character.

That evening we returned to Paris on the helicopter, falling asleep at once. Needless to say, no one felt like having supper.

→><←

While we were shooting *Jefferson*, another of our films, *In Custody*, opened in Paris. It had been adapted from Anita Desai's novel dealing with the systematic destruction of the Urdu language and culture in India. This film had a special significance for me. Urdu is my language and my culture, and therefore a subject very close to my heart, and I had decided to direct it myself—my first feature film as a director. The Indian ambassador to France, Ranjit Sethi, and his charming wife, Indu, offered to host a party in honor of Shashi Kapoor, the star of the film, who would be in Paris. I was asked to submit a guest list, and one of the names on my list was Jeanne Moreau. I had no reason to expect her to come: We did not know each other, and had never even met. But considering that we were both involved in the film industry, and that I spent so much time in France, it seemed odd that our paths had never crossed. Some instinct told me it was time they should.

Contrary to my expectations, Jeanne accepted the invitation. Later she told me that though she generally avoids large social occasions of this kind, some instinct drew her to this one. When we finally met at the Indian Embassy in Paris, we sensed an immediate rapport between us, as though we had known each other all our lives. I told her how I had seen her films in New York when I was a student, and had become determined then and there to make a film with her someday. Would she, I asked, ever consider working with us? Jeanne replied there was no question about it, it was only a matter of finding the right story.

Marc Tissot, a young Swiss actor to whom we had recently been introduced, told me an interesting and somewhat sinister story about the double life of a famous French woman writer, who was then still living. I wasn't interested in pursuing that particular material as the subject of a film, but it occurred to me that Jeanne could play the part of a writer extremely well—few actresses have the ability to convey an inner life with conviction. The idea was so nebulous at that stage that I said nothing to Jeanne about it. However, I was so fired up with enthusiasm for doing a project with Jeanne that I commissioned George Swift Trow to write an original screenplay specifically for her—for a film that, moreover, I intended to direct myself.

I had cut my teeth as a director on *In Custody*; I had also worked at Jim's request as second unit director on both *The Remains of the Day*, where I staged the elaborate banquet preparation in the kitchen of Badminton House, and on *Jefferson in Paris*, where I staged torch-lit fight scenes and Revolutionary riots. I felt confident I could handle one of the great legends of the screen, though some thought me foolhardy to attempt that on only my second film. Still, I was determined. It was like a love affair where both parties think it over carefully before they leap—and then do leap, for better or worse.

Along with the desire to make a film with Jeanne Moreau, the idea of buying a home in Paris had also been brewing for some time. *Jefferson* was the first of four consecutive films we would be making in France and it made practical and economic sense to have a proper base there, rather than moving from one rented apartment to another. While we were making *Jefferson* we had rented an apartment facing the Quai D'Orleans on the Ile St. Louis, conveniently close to the Brasserie de l'Ile St. Louis, which had become one of our regular haunts over the years. Both the apartment and its location were perfect, but I was dismayed, though fascinated, by the landlord's cooking arrangements—the apartment had a tiny kitchen hardly larger than the utility kitchens in New York City apartment buildings, with barely enough room for one person and only a couple of burners to cook on. Yet, apparently this minute kitchen was intended to service the spacious dining area—a room frescoed with happy Parisian scenes in the style of Dufy where everyone sat down to eat off the billiard table. With our six-month lease ending simultaneously with the *Jefferson* shoot, I felt the time had come to either buy or lease a larger property in Paris.

I had, in fact, first seriously considered buying property when we found a duplex apartment in the 15th arrondissement as a location for Jefferson's house in the film. The cost of the rental was so high that it occurred to me I could probably buy a place for that kind of money. Jim, always cautious, warned me of the perils and pitfalls of buying property in a foreign country. So, I immediately started looking for an apartment to buy. As the king told Jefferson, in Paris it's important to find a good house.

The headwaiter of the Brasserie de l'Ile St. Louis at his command post. The hanging white card is advertising the recently arrived Beaujolais Nouveau.

As we would be based in Paris for the foreseeable future it also made sense to establish a permanent office in the city. I had already earmarked for that purpose a large vacant space in Humbert Balsan's office building on rue Montmartre, which had been used to lodge the art department for *Jefferson*. So, in August 1994, we opened offices in Paris and Merchant Ivory France was born—we were now officially French.

The search for a home, however, was not quite so easy. Of the dozens of properties I viewed, most were unsuitable or too expensive, and the few I was interested in somehow slipped from my grasp. Angelo Manzolini, the contractor responsible for creating our office, heard about my search for an apartment and told me of one in the Saint-Germain-des-Prés district on the Left Bank. The apartment had belonged to the trendsetting interior designer Madeleine Castaing, who had died three years earlier on the day before her 98th birthday. It was arranged that I should go and see it. The building, put up partly in the seventeenth century and partly in the eighteenth, had been a large *hotel particulier* and formed a U around a walled courtyard opening on to rue Bonaparte. Now it was broken up into several big apartments on the three floors, with the usual *chambres de bonnes* on top. Everything in Madeleine Castaing's apartment had been left exactly as it was at the time of her death. It was the most extraordinary testament to her unique and iconoclastic style: a mix of fine if rather battered English and French antiques, gilded Chinese trellises, trompe l'oeil, gilt-framed mirrors with red lipstick inscriptions on the glass, and theater props—the place simply defied description.

The apartment had the air of dusty, age-old loss, somewhat like Miss Haversham's moldy house in *Great Expectations*, and, in fact, we learned that Castaing had originally readied the place to move into with a new husband, who then suddenly died. Afterward, she used it as a sort of showroom for her decorating talents. You had to push past disintegrating Victorian overstuffed chairs and little gilt tables with collections of kitsch, and the curtains and window shades fell apart if touched. Here and there on the walls, in the gloom, were paintings by Soutine, who had been Castaing's protegé. But one could see that the apartment, once cleared of its collection of props—props of a decorator, roughly tacked together, for it was the effect that mattered, as on a movie set— was superbly laid out, spacious, and full of light (but also full of noise from the

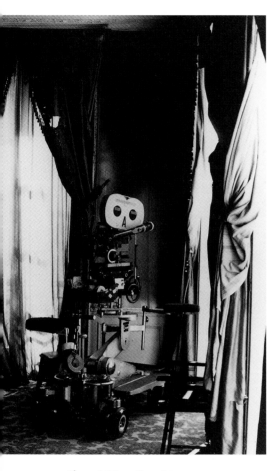

Above: A 35mm Panavision camera in a dilapidated corner of the apartment at 21, rue Bonaparte during the filming of *The Proprietor.*

Opposite: The hallway of the late Madame Castaing's apartment at 21, rue Bonaparte before Merchant Ivory took it over.

busy rue Bonaparte). The floor plan was L-shaped, the classic formal French *enfilade* of room following room, each with two tall windows looking out on the street. The largest rooms all had very fine marble mantelpieces; but, as with all old houses, virtually no closets. Only the kitchen was a disappointment and my heart sank when I first saw it—it was a mere afterthought, a wretchedly equipped hole-in-the-wall.

I knew at once that this was the place for me. It would need extensive restoration, for despite it stylishness and dramatic impact, it had been neglected. But, there was another reason why my response to it had been so immediate, and this is what made its purchase so compelling: I saw it as the perfect location for *The Proprietor,* the film I was planning for Jeanne Moreau. I could shoot the film there, then refurbish the place and move in. I had it all worked out, except for one unexpected detail: Michel Castaing, Madeleine Castaing's son and owner of the apartment, at first refused to sell it to me. He thought I was an American-style film producer who hoped to buy the place for next to nothing, shoot a film there (probably trashing it in the process), and then abandon it.

Nevertheless, I took Jeanne to see the apartment. When she entered she told me she had the most extraordinary feeling about it—a sense that she already knew the place and that it was strangely familiar to her. She seemed disturbed by this inexplicable déjà vu. Later, she realized that she had been to the apartment before: some thirty years earlier Jean Cocteau had taken her to a dinner party there, and Madeleine Castaing had been her hostess.

Monsieur Castaing refused to negotiate, or even meet me, and the situation was further complicated by my having to return to New York. Before I left Paris I asked Marc Tissot, who had begun to work for Merchant Ivory by now, to somehow engineer a meeting with Monsieur Castaing. He was to explain that, though I did indeed intend to shoot a movie in the apartment, my principal reason for buying it was to restore it and live there, because to me it represented something unique. This argument should not necessarily have impressed Castaing, given the extraordinary upheaval that occurs when a film company moves onto a location of this kind, but apparently it did. He must have thought our film would immortalize the image that his mother had created, and that a valuable and instructive record would be seen by millions of cinemagoers. Many people who don't know how movies are made exhibit this type of belief in movie sets, and filmmakers no doubt take advantage of that faith. Tissot was sufficiently persuasive that Monsieur Castaing agreed to negotiate, and by early fall the sale was completed. We lived briefly in the extraordinary setting Madeleine Castaing had created, among her personal possessions, being careful not to overturn the many little tables covered with trinkets, or electrocute ourselves in her bathtub, which had hot wires sticking out of the decorative wall sconces immediately above it.

Through Marc's meeting with Monsieur Castaing, I learned of the apartment's poignant history. Madeleine Castaing bought it in 1960 and spent the next six years refurbishing it, preparing everything down to the last detail. When the apartment was finally completed, on the very day she had planned to move in, her husband died. Madame Castaing did not have the heart to move in after that. Occasionally she would host a dinner party there, or take clients and prospective buyers through, but otherwise the apartment remained unoccupied, kept almost as a shrine, until the last years of her life when her failing health obliged her to live there as a more convenient place to work.

Yet we knew, as Monsieur Castaing knew too, that it was not possible for any buyer to be happy in the atmosphere his mother had created so long ago, with little old stiff-backed chairs that threatened to splinter, musty carpets that you didn't want to walk on in your bare feet, and ancient drains stinking behind the fine old woodwork. All the contents were for sale—except the Soutines, which were expected to go to the auctioneer—but at such exaggerated prices that we felt our good sense had been somewhat insulted. We did buy four or five things, a fine porcelain stove among them, which now takes off the chill in the dining room in the winter. The Castaings had no idea it worked: It had just been another prop, placed on a set to look good.

Jeanne Moreau was excited that I had finally succeeded in buying the apartment and that we would be shooting there. By now it had become the catalyst and a central theme in the story of our film. Jim, who had never doubted for a moment that I would succeed with the purchase, simply treated it as a fait accompli and began to think of ways we could be more comfortable there.

In the months of preproduction work on *The Proprietor*, Jeanne and I spent a great deal of time together, and I was delighted to discover that she shared my passion for food and cooking, and was, in fact, a very accomplished cook. Jeanne loves the whole process of preparing a meal and feeding people, and I believe

Above: Merchant with Jeanne Moreau and Jean-Yves Dubois during filming of *The Proprietor*.

Below: Christopher Cazenove and Jeanne Moreau.

that attitude leads to great cooking. Whenever she invited me to her home, we would go straight to the kitchen where she would prepare something simple and delicious to eat, talking and smoking fiendishly all the while. The first time Jeanne cooked for me she made roast chicken, potato salad, and a *frisée* and endive salad, which may sound prosaic but was a perfect example of how good simple food can be if the ingredients are of the best quality and are prepared properly and imaginatively. Jeanne is not keen on heavy or complicated food, so I had no idea how she would react to my kind of cooking, which, though not complicated, can be quite rich. Fortunately, she loved it, though she often complained that it was so delicious she would eat too much and would then have to diet for a month.

One of Jeanne's favorite restaurants in Paris is Carpaccio at the Hotel Marceau, near her home in the 8th arrondissement. I could see at once why it appealed to her. This Italian restaurant was quietly stylish in design, and the cooking was simple but perfectly executed. Everything about the place was unpretentious and relaxing. As soon as we sat down, the waiter would bring *ciabetta* bread and bowls of olive oil to keep us busy until the first course arrived. Jeanne's favorite pasta was one with a light but powerfully flavored tomato-and-basil sauce. We usually followed this with fish, especially *daurade*, which was grilled with rosemary and lots of lemon and black pepper. Jeanne

Sean Young and Marc Tissot in a scene from *The Proprietor*.

Right: Madame Castaing's sitting room with its porcelain stove. The light fixture probably once hung over a billiard table. One basic of French decorative taste today is to cover walls with cloth rather than paper: The cloth is laid over cotton padding and tacked down. In this room, Mme Castaing eliminated the cloth, featuring the padding instead. After forty years it had sagged into festoons of grime and cobweb, but the effect was still somehow stylish.

The same room today, with the original porcelain stove surrounded by Indian furniture.

Madame Castaing's bedroom as she left it, with a lipstick inscription on the mirror reading "Où vas-tu bellissima?"

A flashback scene in *The Proprietor*, set in Maxim's.

Opposite, above: Stage Two of Merchant's overhaul of his living room—once the dining room—at 21, rue Bonaparte. It has since gone through one more transformation, but looks much the same.

Opposite, below: The same room, shot during a scene of *The Proprietor*, in which Adrienne Mark (Jeanne Moreau) revisits her childhood home.

also introduced me to the Maison du Chocolat, which has the best hot chocolate in the city, particularly the ones made with Grand Marnier or Armagnac.

But there was to be less and less time for these indulgences as shooting of *The Proprietor* approached. We needed to begin shooting by May at the latest, or it would clash with our next film, *Surviving Picasso*, which was scheduled to begin in mid-August. May, however, presented many problems: we would be in Cannes with *Jefferson in Paris*, and Jeanne was committed to doing a film in Germany immediately after the festival, making our schedule even tighter. I knew I was capable of directing *The Proprietor* and producing *Surviving Picasso* without harm to either project, but Jim and Ruth didn't believe me and were growing increasingly concerned about the latter, which had many distracting problems of its own.

Then I learned that Jeanne had been appointed president of the jury at Cannes, and this gave me an idea. The final scenes of *The Proprietor* are set at the Cannes Film Festival—scenes that would be extremely difficult and expensive to stage. As we would be participating in the festival with *Jefferson in Paris*, and as Jeanne would now also be there, I decided to shoot the real event to use in our film—this would cost us next to nothing. Money was no small consideration, as we still hadn't raised any for *The Proprietor* apart from some initial funding from Eurimages. I was once again in the familiar situation of preparing to shoot a film before I had raised the finance for it. *Plus ca change.*

Lighthearted (some might say lightheaded), nevertheless, Jim, our executive producer Donald Rosenfeld, Marc Tissot, and I drove down to Cannes, stopping near Arles to dine and spend the night at l'Oustaù de Baumanière, a five hundred-year-old *mas* in the wild and beautiful *Val d'Enfer*, the Valley of Hell. In keeping with the period, there is no end to the blackened old beams, canopied beds, and shiny brass; but, it was the vaulted dining room and the cooking of Jean-André Charial-Thuiller that particularly drew me. This chef has retained the classical perfection of the traditional Provençal dishes, but has added new flavors and daring combinations of ingredients, an approach to cooking I admire. We ate artichoke hearts with young peas, leg of lamb in puff pastry, and an almond tart with pine nuts. Monsieur Charial-Thuilier's menu is seasonal, and we were fortunate to catch the best of the spring produce. I would like to return in another season to try the sea bass in a salt crust with tarragon sauce, or the chef's famous lamb with olives.

In Cannes I became something of a split personality: producer of *Jefferson in Paris*, which was in competition, and of the upcoming *Surviving Picasso*, which I had to promote, as well as director of *The Proprietor*, which I had to shoot and find financing for. Nick Nolte and Greta Scacchi were there to publicize *Jefferson*, and we had also brought with us the actors involved in the Cannes sequences of *The Proprietor*—Christopher Cazenove, Sean Young, Josh Hamilton, Marc Tissot, and also Jean-Pierre Aumont, who had starred in *Jefferson*. With our two casts in tow, whenever we made our ascent up the Aztec steps of the Palais for an evening show, there was plenty to keep the paparazzi busy, and much to make the festival happy.

In reality, Jeanne was president of the Cannes jury, but for *The Proprietor*, Jeanne was Adrienne, a writer whose contribution to French cinema was being honored at the festival. The lines between fact and fiction were never more blurred than when Jeanne arrived at the opening ceremony as herself—and I was shooting her as Adrienne for the film. Naturally, Jeanne was aware of what I wanted her to do as Adrienne, but she needed to do it covertly while, to all intents and purposes, she was Jeanne Moreau fulfilling her actual festival duties.

My plan to infiltrate the event with my actors and camera crew had seemed simple enough. But even though I had attended the festival many times, now, in my capacity of director, I suddenly became aware of the reality of the situation and the difficulties of trying to shoot in these circumstances. Thousands of people solidly blocked the area around the Palais, banks of photographers were battling with our cameras for space, and we would have only one chance to capture this scene on film—albeit from three different cameras, which provided something of a safety net.

I stood next to Larry Pizer, my collaborator and ever-resourceful cinematographer, on the steps outside the Palais and waited for the official procession escorting the jury to arrive. Jeanne emerged from the first car, smiling radiantly, and as the rest of the jury arrived they assembled around her. Then our cast drove up in the official cars that I had persuaded the person in charge of the festival transport to give us, and they followed Jeanne and the jury up the steps of the Palais ahead of the rest of the guests. To observers, this scene of actors walking up the Palais steps to applause and flashbulbs appeared entirely normal. For me, it represented a million-dollar shot—fabulous production values, stars, a huge, well-dressed crowd, photographers, limousines, authentic atmosphere—and we had managed to contrive it all at virtually no expense.

Although there was some interest in *The Proprietor* from buyers at Cannes, and the money was beginning to come together, there was still a considerable shortfall in the budget. One night, Greta Scacchi, Marc Tissot, and I were invited to a dinner party aboard the yacht of a Saudi Arabian prince, where I met yet another Saudi Arabian prince who invited me aboard *his* yacht. So, a few days later, we found ourselves on board his floating palace where we had cocktails and watched a video of the prince hand-feeding sharks in Jeddah. The prince was interested in film so we discussed cinema in general, but he seemed particularly keen to know more about our work and our organization. I told him about *The Proprietor*, and he asked to see a proposal, which we sent to him the next day. Some weeks later, when I was back in Paris, I had a call from a Zurich banker acting on behalf of the prince, who wanted more information about the film. This was also sent, and after a few days we heard from the banker again—he had been authorized by his client to put up a portion of the budget for *The Proprietor*, and to inform us that his client was also keen to become associated with Merchant Ivory on other projects. Back in 1961, on my first trip to Cannes, I had hoped to find some millionaire who would hand me a check to make a feature film: Thirty years later I had finally found one aboard a splendid yacht.

We resumed shooting of *The Proprietor* in Paris in July, after Jeanne had completed her film in Germany, and I now had to move out of my new home on rue Bonaparte to allow the art department to prepare it for the film. This was undoubtedly some kind of retribution for the many times I have relentlessly badgered people into quitting their homes in order that we might use their premises as a film location. Now, as I packed my suitcases, I began to have some sympathy for those whose homes we had invaded in the past. Not only did I have the inconvenience of relocating, but I also had to watch my home being stripped and put through three separate transformations: the apartment at the time of World War II; the apartment empty and forlorn fifty years later; and the apartment as refurbished by Adrienne Marke after she had bought it and moved in. There was a certain irony in this because the whole purpose of buying a place in Paris had been precisely to avoid needing to camp out from film to film. But, as the apartment had in many ways inspired the film, and as we always try to shoot in authentic locations, I became a victim of our own procedures.

While I had been busy on *The Proprietor*, preproduction work was progressing in Paris on *Surviving Picasso*—an account of the artist's life during the years he was involved with Françoise Gilot—with Anthony Hopkins in the title role. But, with a mere two months left before shooting was due to begin, we faced a serious setback. Claude Picasso, Pablo Picasso's son, and Françoise Gilot, Claude's mother, whom we had hoped would agree to cooperate with us, suddenly withdrew their approval of the film, claiming that we were breaching both copyright and privacy laws.

Although the Picasso heirs had never encouraged filmmakers in the past, nothing had prepared us for such a dramatic standoff. We knew that others—most recently Anthony Quinn—who had tried to make films about Picasso had always met with opposition from the artist's estate. But, Gilot had initially been very enthusiastic about our idea for this film, and we had been delighted to have her blessing bestowed on us over a lunch in the Russian Tea Room in New York. Although we were under no obligation to do so, we had sent Gilot a copy of the script as a gesture of good faith. However, in the meantime Warner Brothers, who had initiated the project—which had originally included Gilot in a writing partnership with Arianna Stassinopoulos-Huffington—became cautious about committing the initial sum of $250,000, which was the amount we had agreed to pay the Picasso estate's representative, the Artists Rights Society, for the rights to use the artist's original work in the film.

Either because of this, or because there may have been some truth in the rumor that Claude Picasso had always intended to make his own film on the life of his father, Gilot suddenly objected to the script, claiming that we had portrayed Picasso as a very flawed character. Gilot's own account of her years with Picasso, published in her autobiography, *Life with Picasso*, is itself highly critical of the artist's tyrannical, even sadistic, nature and is, ultimately, far more damning of him than our script is. Nevertheless, Claude Picasso refused us access to Picasso's works and challenged Warner Brothers' right to make the film at all. The inevitable response from any stouthearted filmmaker to such a provocation can be imagined: I told Claude Picasso that the film would still be made, with or without his permission, and with or without his father's art. Warner Brothers, who had already invested considerable money in the project, took the same position.

Julianne Moore, as Dora Maar, in *Surviving Picasso*.

The press immediately picked up the story, and we read in the paper extensive interviews with Françoise Gilot saying she would try to prevent the film from being made by getting the French courts to bring an injunction against us. France does have very strict privacy laws; but, by writing about her life with Picasso, Gilot herself had chosen to make her private life public so she was on shaky legal ground. In addition, she had been interviewed at great length for the Stassinopoulos book on Picasso, which had then been bought by Warner Brothers, so any rights to privacy had been by then considerably diluted. We decided to ignore the threats and go ahead with the film as planned, even though we knew the Picasso estate would never grant us reproduction rights to the works of art. We read in the newspapers of threats made by Claude Picasso that, if we were to shoot even a single frame of any Picasso art, he would send in the gendarmes to confiscate our film. We decided, therefore, to show no Picassos in the film, and the seven weeks we spent shooting on the Côte d'Azur and in Paris passed calmly. No gendarmes appeared, but the threat of some sort of unspecified legal action hung over us.

For that reason Warner Brothers wanted us to take the precaution of having alternate locations arranged in advance, so that in the event of trouble we could

In a scene from *Surviving Picasso*, Dora Maar (Julianne Moore) confronts her weary rival, Françoise Gilot (Natascha McElhone), in the Café de Flore, which is still a meeting place—as it was in Picasso's day—for writers and artists on the Left Bank.

shift the whole unit to another place with minimal loss of time. As usual, we had chosen to shoot at the authentic locations associated with Picasso in the forties and fifties, but we also drew up contingency plans to shoot just over the border on the Italian coast, out of the jurisdiction of the French authorities. All the Paris interiors would be re-created at Pinewood Studios in England, except for those of the Brasserie Lipp and Café de Flore, two famous establishments on the boulevard Saint Germain that were at the heart of the Left Bank artistic community during Picasso's time. We decided to take that risk because those scenes could be shot briskly and discreetly—by the time Claude Picasso alerted the authorities we would have completed the job and moved on.

There were two scenes in the film, however, that there was no discreet way to shoot, and that would expose us completely: the occupation of Paris by the Nazis, and the subsequent liberation of the city by the Allies. We had intended to shoot those scenes at the Place de la Concorde and the Place Dauphine, right in the center of the city, but now there was a serious risk that, if we did, the gendarmes really would come and stop us. This would be too public a statement of our determination to proceed.

By coincidence, there was also an occupation scene in *The Proprietor*, and this gave us an idea of how we could solve this dilemma. Of all the extraordinary things I have done in the course of my career, I had never before shot two films simultaneously on the same location—but that is exactly what we now planned to do. Under cover of shooting occupation scenes for *The Proprietor*, we would, at the same time, be shooting them for *Surviving Picasso*. Neither the lawyers for Gilot nor the Picasso estate would be aware of it, and therefore, they would be unable to stop it.

At six o'clock on a Sunday morning in late August 1995—the last day we could shoot this scene in the relatively deserted capital before the Parisians returned from their summer vacations—we marched into Place de la Concorde with three cameras, a huge crew, hundreds of extras, and a fleet of period cars and tanks. Of course, if you move Nazi troops into the Place de la Concorde on such a scale, television stations and newspapers from all over report what's going on. The slates for both films that day had *The Proprietor* written on them, which was the truth—though not the whole truth. The battalion of Nazi troops goose-stepping across the Place de la Concorde in time to a marching band, and the liberation army crossing the Pont Neuf, were the most ambitious crowd

scenes we had ever done outside India. What a sight it would have been if they had been stopped by a process server waving a paper!

While we were shooting the New York sequences of *The Proprietor*, the refurbishment of my apartment was completed, and when I returned from America I would finally move in. I was now part of a French community, an official resident of Saint-Germain-des-Prés, an area that represents something more than a geographical location or a postal code. For more than a century, writers, artists, and men and women of letters have gravitated here—their ghosts haunt the cobbled labyrinthine streets and busy boulevards, and their names are recalled on the many plaques placed on the house fronts. This is the intellectual heart of the city, a melting pot of new ideas continuously emerging from the shadows of the Sorbonne and the *Grandes Écoles*. And while these noble seats of learning, the great libraries, and the local bookshops and galleries feed one's cultural appetites and one's soul, less than a ten-minute walk from my apartment the glorious market of rue de Buci satisfies one's corporeal needs.

I first visited this market when we were shooting *Quartet*, never imagining that one day I would be paying a daily visit, picking up warm croissants from the bakery and taking them back to my own apartment for breakfast. This tiny narrow

In a scene from *Surviving Picasso*, Parisians in the Place Dauphine burn the Nazi flag on Liberation Day in August 1944.

street has absolutely everything: *boulangeries* and pâtisseries; a fishmonger with an extraordinary variety of fish, shellfish, and seafood; cheese shops; wine merchants; and butchers specializing in red meat, game birds, tripe, or poultry, each one preparing his cuts with the precision of a surgeon. There are fruit and vegetable stalls piled high with seasonal produce; charcuteries specializing in the foods of Alsace (stuffed cabbage, for example) and the Auvergne (mouth-watering cassoulet); a brilliant florist who incorporates fruit and vegetables into his imaginative bouquets; an excellent *traiteur* with an ever-changing variety of take-out dishes; and sidewalk *rôtisseries* filling the air with the aroma of crispy, spit-roasted chicken. And then, of course, there are cafés, restaurants, bars, and brasseries.

Every shop spills out onto the pavement and into the street to the point that pedestrians have to maneuver gingerly between the stalls to avoid the motorists who do not seem to regard the blocked street as an impediment to driving. Summer and winter, the market operates from early morning until well into the evening. At night, the street is ablaze with light, and still alive with shoppers. However late I finish work in the office or on the set, I know I can come here and pick up wonderful ingredients to cook at home. No wonder supermarkets, with their plastic-wrapped food and sterile, soulless atmosphere, have never caught on in Paris.

No sooner had the last "cut" been called on *The Proprietor*, than the first "action" was called on *Surviving Picasso*, code-named "Film Nineteen" for the duration of our shooting—part of the whole cloak-and-dagger scenario we felt we had to adopt in order to make this film. We shot at undisclosed locations, denied all access to the press, maintained a very low profile, and managed to elude trouble completely.

With each passing day I kept hoping, perversely, that the gendarmes *would* descend, brandishing their batons. I was somehow disappointed that it never happened and that I would not be at the center of one of those peculiarly French cultural causes célèbres, which would have given me the opportunity to say what was on my mind about this affair.

While we were filming the Côte d'Azur sequences in the south of France, we rented a wonderful house in Giens. The house had a huge galleried dining room with a round table that could easily accommodate twenty people. An opportunity not to be missed, I telephoned Jeanne Moreau and invited her to come down from Paris for a few days. Inevitably, we spent much time in the

Above: Merchant considers the fruit at a stall in the rue de Buci market.

Below: A florist in the rue de Buci market.

kitchen producing our Franco–Indian meals: I would be in one corner cooking rice fragrant with spices and herbs, or stirring a pot of steaming dal; Jeanne would be in the other performing her special magic with chicken and peppercorns, or making *pâte de pomme*, the best potato dish I have ever eaten. An old Moreau family recipe that Jeanne learned from her father, she cooked this dish on the night we invited about fourteen people to dinner, and Anthony Hopkins, Jane Lapotaire, and Natascha McElhone were as taken with Jeanne's *pâte de pomme* as I had been.

→>-<←

Nearly every film I have ever made has involved intense battles for financing because the kind of work we do does not immediately signal substantial box office returns to investors. That we have survived in this business for more than three decades indicates there is an audience for intelligent films, yet this still counts for nothing with many financiers and distributors. They cannot imagine that we could have a success with unlikely material; yet our greatest successes *were* unlikely. When we originally tried to present to financiers what have turned out to be our best stories, such as *A Room with a View* and *Heat and Dust*, they just shook their heads. Our latest film, *A Soldier's Daughter Never Cries*—based on the semiautobiographical novel by Kaylie Jones about her father, the author James Jones—was written off by everyone in Hollywood because it was not considered sufficiently commercial. Nor were our stars, Barbara Hershey and Kris Kristofferson, deemed sufficiently bankable. However, an actor's bankability has always been less relevant to us than his or her suitability for the role.

After tremendous struggles that involved waiving my salary and putting up one million dollars of the company's money as collateral, I finally managed to put the seven-million-dollar budget together. We had already begun shooting by then—a familiar situation for us. However, as soon as the last agreements were signed, I put the unpleasant experiences and time-wasting tactics of the agents, lawyers, and unhelpful investors behind me. I wanted to enjoy what was to be, at least for the present, our last French-based film—for our next projects will take us far away from Paris to Trinidad, South India, and England.

A Soldier's Daughter Never Cries began for us in 1991, but it was postponed until we could fulfill our previous film commitments to Columbia,

Disney, and Warner Brothers with the films *Remains of the Day*, *Jefferson in Paris*, and *Surviving Picasso*. *A Soldier's Daughter* became our fourth film in a row set in France. We found we had gradually put together a production team there that was as efficient as those we had in England and America. We had access to wonderful new film technicians and dedicated craftsmen who wanted to work for us, and Jim and I began to feel thoroughly at home in France. Paris, a city that had initially attracted us because of its beauty and many pleasures, had now also become a place to work hard in, like New York in some ways, where people work all the time and think not of the hours put in, but of the well-made finished product.

For me, one of the greatest pleasures of working on this film was that it involved shooting in locations I knew well, such as the Brasserie de l'Ile St. Louis. Coincidentally, James Jones had also gone there frequently when he lived on the Ile St. Louis. As a regular customer of the Brasserie for almost forty years, I never doubted that the owners, Michele Kappe and her mother, Marthe Guepratte, would give us permission to shoot there, especially as they remembered James Jones well. But my emissaries came back with a very firm refusal. I went to see the owners myself and had a long discussion with Mesdames Kappe and Guepratte: I even attempted the intercession of Ange "Gino" Allano, the waiter who had served me so many times over the years. But the ladies were adamant. They told me they received so many requests from film producers that if they allowed me to shoot in their popular brasserie it would set a precedent and make it harder to refuse the others.

Of course, it was quite obvious why the Brasserie should be in such great demand as a film location. It has a potent authenticity because it has never been modernized or spruced up. The worn wooden floors, the ancient paintwork ingrained with nicotine, and the battered antique chrome coffee machine all suggest another era. No one could remember when the place had last received a fresh coat of paint—certainly not since I had been going there. But the Brasserie represented more than just a location for us, it was a place James Jones and his cronies had frequented. Mesdames Kappe and Guepratte, however, shook their heads: The restaurant would be out of action while we filmed and that would inconvenience their customers.

I argued that the Brasserie is closed all day Wednesday and I was sure we

Above: The vibrant new French actress Virginie Ledoyen on the beach at Cabourg in Normandy in the opening scene of *A Soldier's Daughter Never Cries.* 1997.

Left: Bênoit (Samuel Gruen). adopted by the American Willis family. arriving at his new home in Paris shepherded by a social worker (Marie Henriau).

could get all our shooting done in that time, plus the morning of Thursday—not much of a disruption to their normal business hours. Still, they hesitated. So, on top of the location fee, which in itself would be substantial, I offered them a trip to India as my guests. Mesdames Kappe and Guepratte exchanged the kind of looks that suggested they thought I was mad. Then they said that of all the inducements they had ever been offered, this was the craziest, so—they had to accept! I was delighted—not only because the Brasserie was essential to the film, but because it held such personal resonance for me.

We faced similar resistance from the Palais Garnier, where we wanted to film our own staging of Strauss's *Salome*. Now superseded as the premier opera house in France by the new Opera Bastille, the Garnier, with its monumental architecture and extravagant *belle époque* halls, is still one of the finest showpieces of Second Empire Paris. The spectacular sweep of its broad marble staircase flanked by onyx balustrades and bronze nymphs clasping outsized candelabra, and its auditorium ceiling painted by Chagall are breathtaking. Again, disruption of service to the public was given as a reason, with the unwillingness of the stagehands' union, whose members would be required to work on a Sunday, cited as an additional cause for the refusal.

The Indian Ambassador to France, Ranjit Sethi, at whose house I had first met Jeanne Moreau, was on good terms with Hugues Gall, the general director of the Garnier, and he offered to intercede on our behalf. By coincidence, the daughter of the American conductor James Conlon, who regularly conducted at the Garnier, was playing a large part in our film, and he too offered to try to help us. Faced with this two-pronged diplomatic and musical pressure, Monsieur Gall relented and agreed to allow us in. We solved the problem of the stagehands' union by offering never to raise the curtain, but to perform the opera on the stage apron in front of it instead—a visual bit of trickery of which the film's audience will not be aware.

Toward the end of shooting I was contacted by Nocturnes Indiens, a small independent film festival in Lyons dedicated to Indian films. This was their third year of operation and they wanted to screen *Heat and Dust*, *In Custody*, and *Gaatch*, a documentary made by the French director Catherine Berge and produced by my nephew Nayeem Hafizka, about the Bengali actor Soumitra Chatterjee, who had appeared in many of Satyajit Ray's films. I admired the zeal

Madame Guepratte (left) and her daughter Michele Kappe, owners of the Brasserie de l'Ile St. Louis.

of these young Lyonnais for putting on a festival with such an esoteric theme in an industrial French city whose population includes only eight Indian families.

Catherine Berge, Nayeem, my old friend Anna Kythreotis, and I took the TGV, the fast "bullet" train, to Lyons from Paris, arriving within two hours. Annick Charlety, a friend of mine in Paris, had recommended we lunch at Pierre Orsi, a two-star Michelin restaurant in the center of the city. By the time we had been met at the station by the festival representatives and taken to the hotel to drop off our bags, we arrived at the restaurant more than an hour late for our reservation. The maître d' couldn't have been more gracious, however, merely asking us not to linger too long over the menu as the kitchen would soon be closed. This was easier said than done as the menu warranted a great deal of attention. The maître d' suggested some of the specialties of the house, starting with ravioli of foie gras in port and truffles, followed by sea bass with leeks, and finally, a savarin with fig compote. As we were in Burgundy, I chose a Pouilly Fuissé 1985, a white wine with a deep smoky bouquet that complemented the food perfectly.

Little *amuses-bouches* were brought to the table to intrigue us until the serious food arrived, and at the end of this magnificent meal our table was heaped with petits fours, fresh fruit, dried fruit, and chocolates. We nibbled at these as we lingered over coffee and dessert wine, admiring the calm elegance of the dining room, sparkling in all its silver and crystal and abundant with extravagant floral displays. What impresses one so much about French restaurants of this kind is the attention to detail that exists on every level. Because of France's cultural tradition of fine dining, and the importance the French place on the preparation and consumption of food, there is a profound seriousness in the way it is presented and served. An attitude of communion exists between the chefs, waiters, and consumers, not unlike that which exists between the celebrant of the Mass, his silent assistants, and the communicants in the church.

As we were leaving I was about to ask for the bill when Nayeem, my nephew, winked broadly at me, nudged me in the ribs and whispered conspiratorially that the festival was taking care of it. This seemed unlikely to me; I knew that the festival was strapped for money, existing with minimal sponsorship and no government subsidy. Nayeem seemed so confident about it, however, that I was about to sail blithely out of the place when the maître d' discreetly brought

In a scene from *A Soldier's Daughter Never Cries*, Bill Willis (Kris Kristofferson), based on the writer James Jones, and his daughter Channe Willis (Lele Sobieski), based on Kaylie Jones, play pinball in the Brasserie de l'Ile St. Louis.

what turned out to be a very large bill to my attention. Once outside, I pointed out to Nayeem that, had he used his head, it might have occurred to him that underfunded film festivals rarely entertain their guests in Michelin-starred restaurants. But this admonishment would have carried more weight had I not been laughing so hard at what the awful consequences—not to mention bad publicity—might have been had our party actually left without paying the colossal bill.

We walked back to the hotel along the pleasant boulevards and took in some of the city that had inspired the Lumière brothers at the outset of cinematography. Lyons is where the movies began, and that night I was delighted to see a cinema packed with a young enthusiastic crowd for the screening of my film *In Custody*. Afterward I made a short speech and answered questions from the audience. Although my grasp of the French language was improving all the time, and my vocabulary was increasing, I was far from mastering the grammar and pronunciation and I felt this lack particularly keenly that night; I so much wanted to communicate properly with this bright and lively audience. I got by, but it was frustrating not to be able to articulate my thoughts properly. It made me regret flunking out of my French classes at the Sorbonne, for that is what had recently happened.

I had not yet achieved my last ambition in France. I had always wanted to live and work and make films in France, and I had done that. But I had also wanted to study at the Sorbonne and learn to speak French fluently. So, at the beginning of the autumn term of 1997, I enrolled at the Sorbonne to study French literature and civilization. Although we had just begun to shoot *A Soldier's Daughter Never Cries*, and the demands on my time were very tight, I felt it was now or never. Our future films would take me to America, England, and India, and although I would still be coming to Paris regularly, I had no idea when I would be able to spend any length of time there again. This could be the last opportunity I would have, for a long time, to fulfill my dream. On paper it all seemed possible: classes from eight until ten each morning, and then on with my usual routine for the rest of the day.

I arrived late for my first interview at the Sorbonne because I was held up on the set. This should have been a warning that the life of a student and the demands of producing films are not easily compatible. I was told that I would

The tree house that is featured in the first of the three stories making up *A Soldier's Daughter Never Cries* with its three child actors: Samuel Gruen on the ground; Luisa Conlon on the ladder; and Frédèrick Da on the deck.

have to take a written test. I was a little nervous, because a written test would be very difficult for me. Nevertheless, I "passed" and was accepted. In this case, "passing" must have meant that my grade was so poor, the only logic was to strive to improve, so I was "passed" into the beginner's class.

On the first day of the semester I took my exercise books and pencils and walked to the Sorbonne from my apartment, feeling excited about going back to school, even at age sixty. The rest of the students in my class were in their teens and early twenties, and they regarded me with great curiosity. We each had to introduce ourselves by giving our name, nationality, and age. When my turn came, I stood up and announced that my name was Ismail Merchant, I came from India, and I was—young. Everyone laughed. I explained it is one's spirit, rather than one's years, that is important for learning, and in spirit I felt no older than my classmates. The lesson went very well, and I returned the following day more eager than ever. But the rest of that day was consumed with negotiations, meetings, telephone calls, and visits to the set, and somehow I never got around to doing my homework. When I returned on the third day, my professor, cane in hand, scolded me severely for not preparing the lesson. I was eight years old again—a naughty schoolboy who had neglected his work. On the fourth day I couldn't turn up at all because I had to go to London for meetings with the bankers of the film—and then somehow the film took over my life entirely and I dropped out of school.

But I am not discouraged, and one day I intend to take a full three months—maybe even longer—away from filming to resume my academic studies in France seriously. So, this is not the end of the dream. I will be back because I still have unfinished business with irregular verbs and compound tenses. I would also like to speak French at least as well as Jim, who throws around expressions like *alors* and *et puis* and *au fond* but, maddeningly, cannot remember the French words for key, stove, and bank deposit. Until then I will continue to communicate in my own syntax-free zone, as I have always done, hoping there will be no serious mishaps. For, in the really important matters—filming, feasting, and friendships—the French and I have no trouble understanding each other.

The Pont des Arts, Paris.

"Retracing my steps at night as I cross this wooden footbridge on my way home from the office, I often think how lucky I am, and how extraordinary it is, that I am sometimes able to live in this beautiful city. I ask myself: 'How did it ever come about?' And I know Jim asks himself the same question."

—ISMAIL MERCHANT

RECIPES

15 BASIC FRENCH RECIPES

ROAST LEG OF LAMB
Gigot d'agneau

1 leg of lamb, 5 to 6 pounds,
    trimmed of fat

1 garlic clove, cut in slivers

2½ tablespoons oil

5 tablespoons salt

2 onions, thinly sliced

2 carrots, thinly sliced

½ to ¾ pint beef or chicken stock

½ teaspoon lemon juice

Salt

Freshly ground black pepper

Preheat the oven to 500°. Make about 8 quarter-inch incisions on the fatty side of the meat and insert a sliver of garlic into each incision. Brush the leg with oil on all sides, and pat the salt all over it. Place the meat on a rack in a shallow roasting tin and cook it uncovered for about 20 minutes. Reduce the heat to 375°, scatter the vegetables around the rack, and cook for a further 40 to 60 minutes, depending on how well you want it done. Transfer the lamb to a heated dish.

This can be served as it is, or with a sauce made from the accompanying vegetables.

FOR THE SAUCE:

Skim off the fat from the roasting tin, add the stock to the vegetables, and boil on top of the stove for about 5 minutes, stirring frequently. Strain the sauce through a fine sieve and extract as much liquid from the vegetables as possible. Skim the sauce of any surface fat, season with lemon juice, salt and pepper, and serve with the lamb.

SERVES 6 TO 8

BEEF BOURGUIGNON
Boeuf Bourguignon

Heat the oil in a heavy pot or casserole and add the chopped vegetables. Add the meat and cook over a high heat for 5 to 6 minutes, stirring frequently.

Add the salt, pepper, bouquet garni, and red wine. Bring to a boil, then reduce the heat to a gentle simmer. Cover, and cook gently for about 3 hours.

Blend the butter with the flour and incorporate some of the cooking liquid into it. Use this to thicken the stew, stirring well until it is blended. Cook uncovered for 10 more minutes. Sprinkle with parsley before serving.

SERVES 6 TO 8

3 tablespoons oil

2 sticks of celery, finely chopped

2 carrots, finely chopped

2 onions, finely chopped

3 pounds of beef suitable for braising, cut into 2-inch cubes

Salt

Freshly ground black pepper

A bouquet garni of 1 bay leaf, 1 thyme sprig, 5 parsley sprigs

1 bottle of good quality red Burgundy wine

2 tablespoons butter

$\frac{1}{2}$ cup flour

2 teaspoons chopped parsley

SAINT-GERMAIN SOUP
Potage Saint-Germain

Chop the green part of the leeks and put them in a large saucepan with the marrowfat peas, the roughly chopped lettuce and spinach leaves, the chervil, 5 tablespoons of the butter, salt, sugar, and one cup of cold water. Bring to a boil, then lower the heat, cover the saucepan with a soup plate of cold water for a lid, and simmer for 40 minutes. Sieve the contents of the pan. Add the remaining 3 cups of water, which should be lukewarm, and stir until it comes to the boil. Meanwhile, heat the new peas in a new saucepan. Remove the saucepan with the marrowfat peas from the heat, add the remaining butter and the heated new peas.

SERVES 6 TO 8

2 leeks

4 cups marrowfat peas

12 lettuce leaves, chopped

12 spinach leaves, chopped

1 teaspoon chervil, chopped

1 stick butter

2 teaspoons salt

4 teaspoons sugar

1 quart water

1 cup small new peas

124

RED MULLET WITH FENNEL
Rougets au fenouil

6 red mullet, cleaned and scaled, but
    with their livers

Salt

Pepper

3 fennel bulbs

4 tablespoons fine white bread crumbs

1 tablespoon butter, softened, plus extra

2 tablespoons olive oil

Remove the livers from the fish, and season fish and livers with salt and pepper.

Remove the tough outer layers of the fennel bulbs, cutting off any fine green leaves and chopping them into a bowl. Quarter the fennel bulbs, and simmer in salted water until almost tender. Remove them and keep the water. Preheat the oven to 375º.

Chop 4 fennel quarters and add to the bowl of fennel leaves. Slice the rest of the fennel and spread in a layer over the bottom of a buttered ovenproof dish large enough to hold the mullet in a single layer. Add the bread crumbs, softened butter, and over a tablespoon of oil to the chopped fennel, moistening the mixture with a little of the fennel cooking water. Add the chopped livers to this mixture, stir, and stuff the fish with it. Any leftover mixture can go with the sliced fennel on the bottom of the dish.

Put the stuffed mullet into the dish. Dribble the remaining oil over and season. Bake in the oven for 15 minutes.

SERVES 6

CHICKEN IN CURRY SAUCE
Poulet a l'Indienne

1 ½ tablespoons oil

1 ½ tablespoons butter

1 3-pound chicken, cut into 6 pieces

Salt

Freshly ground black pepper

1 onion, thinly sliced

1 clove garlic, crushed

1 tablespoon flour

1 teaspoon coriander powder

½ inch freshly ground or grated ginger

Pinch of cayenne

1 cup chicken stock

Pinch of saffron

Heat the oil and butter in a pan. Season the chicken with salt and pepper and add to the pan, brown the chicken on both sides. Remove the chicken from the pan.

Add the sliced onion and cook until soft but not brown. Add the garlic, flour, coriander powder, ginger, and cayenne and cook, while stirring, for 2 minutes. Return the chicken pieces to the pan. Add the stock, saffron, and a little salt, cover, and simmer for 20 to 25 minutes until the chicken is tender.

Remove the chicken from the pan onto a heated dish. The juice remaining in the pan should be no more than 5 to 6 tablespoons. Reduce if necessary, then spoon over the chicken pieces.

SERVES 4

VICHY CARROTS
Carottes Vichy

Bring the carrots, stock, butter, sugar, salt, and a little pepper to a boil over a moderate heat. Boil briskly in an uncovered pan for about 20 minutes. The carrots should be tender, and the liquid should be reduced to about a tablespoon. Transfer the carrots to a heated dish, and sprinkle with the chopped parsley and freshly ground black pepper.

SERVES 4 TO 6

10 to 12 medium-sized carrots, scraped and cut into $\frac{1}{4}$-inch slices

$1\frac{1}{2}$ cups beef or chicken stock

2 tablespoons butter

5 teaspoons sugar

$\frac{1}{2}$ teaspoon salt

Freshly ground black pepper

2 tablespoons finely chopped fresh parsley

GREEN BEANS IN CREAM
Haricots verts à la crème

Plunge the beans into a large saucepan of salted, boiling water and boil until they are cooked but still very firm. Drain and rinse in cold water.

Preheat the oven to 350°. Butter an ovenproof dish and pile on the beans in layers. Cover with the cream. Add pepper. Cook in the oven for about 20 minutes, until the cream has reduced slightly and begun to thicken.

SERVES 6

2 pounds green beans, trimmed, with strings removed

Butter

$1\frac{1}{2}$ cups crème fraîche, or double cream

PROVENÇAL SUMMER VEGETABLE STEW
Ratatouille

1 large aubergine, about 1½ pounds cut into 1-inch cubes

2 tablespoons sea salt

5 tablespoons olive oil (you may need more)

3 yellow or red bell peppers, cored, seeded, cut into 1-inch strips, then halved

4 small zucchini, cut into 1-inch slices

2 onions, chopped

4 garlic cloves, finely chopped

5 tomatoes, peeled, cored, seeded, and cut into 1-inch slices

2 bay leaves

3 tablespoons chopped parsley

½ teaspoon fresh thyme leaves, chopped

Freshly ground pepper

1 to 2 tablespoons red wine vinegar

20 basil leaves

Put the aubergine pieces in a colander and sprinkle with the salt. Leave to drain for 30 minutes, then rinse and pat dry with paper towels.

Heat 2 tablespoons of olive oil in a large heavy casserole. Add the aubergine and brown on all sides. Remove and put aside. Add another tablespoon of oil to the pan and sauté the bell peppers until they begin to wilt. Remove and put aside. Add the zucchini and sauté until lightly browned. Remove and put aside. Add a few more tablespoons of olive oil to the pan and sauté the onions and garlic over a medium heat until translucent. Add the tomatoes, bay leaves, parsley, thyme, and black pepper and cook for 20 minutes. Return the vegetables to the casserole and cook for 10 minutes. Season with salt, pepper, and vinegar.

Serve at room temperature, garnished with basil leaves.

SERVES 6

CHICKEN WITH BELL PEPPERS BASQUE STYLE
Poulet Basquaise

⅓ cup olive oil

1 large onion, chopped

4 garlic cloves, finely chopped

2 green bell peppers, seeded and sliced

2 red bell peppers, seeded and sliced

6 ripe tomatoes, peeled, seeded, and chopped

2 bay leaves

1 thyme sprig

Salt

Freshly ground black pepper

1 3-pound chicken, cut into 8 pieces

In a deep pan, heat a little less than half the oil and sauté the onion and garlic until they soften but do not brown. Add the bell peppers and toss for about half a minute, then add the tomatoes, herbs, salt, and pepper. Reduce the heat, cover, and let simmer for 20 minutes.

In another pan, heat the rest of the oil and brown the chicken pieces. This will take about 15 to 20 minutes. Pour the cooked peppers with their sauce over the chicken. Cover and simmer for 20 minutes more.

Remove the chicken pieces to a warm dish. Check the sauce for seasoning, and remove the herbs. Spoon the sauce over the chicken.

SERVES 4 TO 6

JOHN DORY WITH FENNEL
Saint-Pierre au fenouil

Clean the fish and make several incisions on each side of them. Brush with olive oil and grill them for about 5 minutes on each side. Place the fennel on a large metal dish, and over it put a metal rack or grid. Lay the fish on the rack. Set the fennel on fire and continue cooking the fish in this way for several minutes, turning it so that both sides become perfumed with the fennel.

SERVES 4

4 small John Dory fish

Olive oil

2 cups dried fennel

MUSHROOM SALAD
Salade de champignons

Wipe and peel the mushrooms and cut off their stalks. Put the mushrooms in a saucepan and sprinkle them with salt and cayenne pepper. Pour in the lemon juice. Add the olive oil, bayleaf, and thyme. Put a tight lid on the saucepan and place over a very low heat (or in a slow oven) for 30 minutes. Allow to cool. Mix well, but gently, so that the mushrooms keep their shape.

SERVES 4

$\frac{1}{2}$ pound mushrooms

Salt

Pinch cayenne pepper

2 tablespoons lemon juice

2 tablespoons olive oil

1 bayleaf

1 sprig thyme

CELERIAC SALAD
Céleri-rave rémoulade

Cut up the celeriac into tiny matchsticks. Mix the olive oil, wine vinegar, salt, and pepper together and pour over the celeriac. Leave to marinate for 8 hours.

Meanwhile, take the hard-boiled egg yolks and cream them with the raw egg yolk and mustard. Then add the olive oil drop by drop, as if making mayonnaise. When all the oil has been added, stir a tablespoon of wine vinegar into the sauce. Drain the celeriac, and cover with the rémoulade sauce.

SERVES 4

2 small (or 1 large) celeriac roots

2 tablespoons olive oil

1 tablespoon wine vinegar

$\frac{1}{2}$ teaspoon salt

White pepper

FOR THE RÉMOULADE SAUCE

2 hard-boiled eggs

1 egg yolk

1 tablespoon mustard

1 cup olive oil

1 tablespoon wine vinegar

CHICKEN IN RED WINE
Coq au vin

6 mushrooms

2 slices of bacon

6 small onions

2 tablespoons butter

1 chicken, preferably a rooster

3 teaspoons olive oil

1 tablespoon flour

1 bottle of good red wine (Chambertin
is very good for this dish)

3 garlic cloves, chopped

Salt

Black pepper

Slice the mushrooms and the bacon and fry them with the onions in the butter until they are lightly browned. Joint the chicken and fry it gently in the olive oil. Add the mushrooms, onions, and bacon pieces to the chicken. Strain all the fat into a saucepan, mix a tablespoon of flour with it and stir till brown. Add a bottle of good red wine to the fat mixture, slowly, stirring as you add it. Put the chicken, mushrooms, onions, bacon, garlic, salt and pepper into the wine sauce. Stir well, bring to a boil, cover, and let simmer for 25 to 30 minutes before serving.

SERVES 6

BEETS WITH FRESH TARRAGON
Betterave à l'estragon

8 medium-sized beets

FOR THE VINAGRETTE

1 tablespoon Dijon mustard

3 tablespoons tarragon vinegar

Two dozen whole leaves of fresh, sweet
tarragon

1 pinch cayenne pepper

Salt

Freshly ground pepper

$3/4$ cup extra virgin olive oil

Remove the tops and roots from the beets. Steam them until they can be pierced with a fork; beets should be firm. Meanwhile, wash and dry the tarragon leaves, and mix the mustard, vinegar, tarragon leaves, cayenne pepper, salt, and pepper in a bowl and whisk well. Slowly add the olive oil, stirring constantly. When the beets are steamed, quarter them, pour over the vinaigrette, and serve hot. For those who like fresh beet leaves and stems, steam with the beets, chop, and add to dish (in which case you may wish to increase the number of tarragon leaves).

This dish is also good as a cold salad. After steaming beets, let them cool, and chop into fine slices. Toss with the vinaigrette and serve.

SERVES 4

ISMAIL MERCHANT'S OWN RECIPES

ISMAIL'S INSTANT APPLE TARTS

This is a virtually instant version of the irresistible *tartes aux pommes* found in every French pâtisserie.

Heat the oven to 220° and place a baking tray in the oven.

Divide the pastry into four pieces, and roll each piece into a circle a little larger than the circumference of the apples.

Cut the apples in half, remove the cores, and slice each half thinly. Put half an apple in the center of each piece of pastry and crimp the pastry edges. Brush the tarts with a little melted butter and sprinkle with sugar.

Grease the heated baking tray, place the tarts on it, and bake for 15 minutes, or until the pastry is cooked. Remove from the oven, brush the tarts with the jam (which may need to be melted) and return to the oven for a further 5 minutes. Cool.

Serve with crème fraîche or whipped cream.

SERVES 4

8 ounces ready-made puff pastry
2 large apples, peeled and cored
2 tablespoons butter
1 tablespoon sugar
4 tablespoons apricot jam
crème fraîche or whipped cream

ISMAIL'S TROPICAL DAURADE (SEA BREAM)

Clean the fish and put it in an ovenproof dish. Mix the next four ingredients and pour over the fish. Add a little salt, and bake in the oven at 375° for 40 minutes.

SERVES 2

1 daurade (sea bream), about $1\frac{1}{2}$ pounds
1 can coconut milk
$\frac{1}{4}$ cup olive oil
12 to 14 crushed black peppercorns
12 whole cloves
Salt

ISMAIL'S INCREDIBLY INSTANT CHICKEN

1 tablespoon olive oil

Salt

1 tablespoon crushed black pepper

1 teaspoon garlic purée or crushed garlic

2 chicken breast fillets, slightly flattened

Juice of half a lemon

1 teaspoon chopped chervil

This dish was created after a particularly long and busy day during the shooting of A Soldier's Daughter Never Cries. *I had been working nonstop since dawn, and when I finally returned home late that night, I was tired and extremely hungry. I wanted something quick and light. This took less time than a sandwich to prepare, and is much more delicious.*

Put the oil in a pan over a medium flame and add the salt, pepper, and garlic purée. Then add the chicken breasts and lemon juice. Cover the pan, and increase the heat. After five minutes turn the chicken fillets over, cover again, and let cook for another 5 to 7 minutes. Sprinkle with fresh chervil before serving.

SERVES 2

ISMAIL'S INDO–PROVENÇAL RICE

6 cups water

1/2 stick butter

A few cinnamon sticks

12 fresh mint leaves (other herbs can be substituted for mint)

1/2 red onion, sliced

6 cups basmati rice

Put the water in a pot with the butter, cinnamon sticks, fresh mint, and sliced onion. Bring the water to a boil, then add the rice and simmer for half an hour.

SERVES 6

ISMAIL'S CORIANDER AND CARDAMOM DRUMSTICKS

1 red onion

1 cup olive oil

12 cardamom pods

12 cloves

1 teaspoon fresh coriander chutney

1 teaspoon garlic purée

1/2 teaspoon salt

1 1/2 teaspoons coarsely ground black pepper

16 chicken legs

1 cup water

Chop the onion and in a large pan sauté in the oil with the cardamom and cloves until it begins to brown. Add the chutney, garlic purée, salt, and pepper and mix well. Then add the chicken drumsticks. Remove the cardamom seeds from the pods and sprinkle over the drumsticks. Add water to the pan, and let the drumsticks cook over a low heat for 30 to 40 minutes.

SERVES 4

ISMAIL'S FRANCO–INDIAN DAURADE

Clean the fish and put it in an ovenproof dish. Mix the garlic, chili powder, olive oil, wine vinegar, and mustard together into a paste and completely cover the fish with it, making sure to fill the cavity as well. Add a little salt, and bake in the oven at 375° for 40 to 45 minutes.

SERVES 2

1 daurade (sea bream), about 1½ pounds

1 teaspoon garlic purée or crushed garlic

1 teaspoon red chili powder

2 tablespoons olive oil

1 teaspoon wine vinegar

1 teaspoon Dijon mustard

Salt

ISMAIL'S CHICORY-AND-DILL SALAD

Separate the chicory leaves, and snip the dill into pieces. Add the oil, lemon juice, and salt and toss well.

SERVES 4

3 heads of chicory

6 twigs of dill

2 tablespoons walnut oil

Juice of ½ lemon

Salt

ISMAIL'S INCREDIBLY FRENCH BEANS

Top and tail the beans but leave them whole. Soak them in very cold water for 5-6 minutes.

Drain the beans and steam them in a vegetable steamer for about 5 minutes or until just tender. Alternatively, cook them in boiling water for 5 minutes. It is important not to overcook them.

Slice the onion into very fine slices, and set aside. Spoon the mustard into a small bowl and add salt, pepper, and lemon juice. Stir to blend, then whisk in the oil. Drain the beans. Add the sliced onions, capers, and mustard sauce to them, and toss to coat well. Serve immediately.

SERVES 4 TO 6

1 pound green beans

1 large red onion

1 tablespoon Dijon mustard

Salt

Freshly ground black pepper

1 to 1½ tablespoons lemon juice

4 tablespoons olive oil

2 tablespoons capers

RECIPES FROM FRENCH RESTAURANTS

L'Oustaù de Baumanière
Les–Baux–de–Provence

POTATO PURÉE WITH OLIVE OIL
Purée de pommes de terre à l'huile d'olive

1¾ pounds baking potatoes
2 tablespoons unsalted butter
1 cup hot crème fraîche
½ cup extra virgin olive oil
Salt

Peel the potatoes and quarter them. Rinse and cook in boiling salted water. When they are cooked, drain them well and sieve, then mash or blend them to a purée.

Add the butter and beat with a wooden spoon until smooth. Stir in the hot crème fraîche and olive oil, season with salt, and serve immediately.

SERVES 4

ROAST DUCK WITH OLIVES
Canard aux olives

FOR THE STOCK
2 carrots
1 onion
1 shallot
1 clove garlic
1 leek
1 stalk celery
½ stick butter
2 cups red wine
2 cups water

1 4-pound oven-ready duck
⅔ cup black olives (with pits)
⅔ cup green olives (with pits)
2 cups Madeira
Salt
Freshly ground black pepper

TO MAKE THE STOCK:
Peel the carrots, onion, shallot, and garlic clove. Wash the leek and celery. Dice them all into fine pieces.

Remove the giblets from the duck as well as the neck, wing tips, and feet. Chop these into small pieces, putting the liver to one side.

Put 2 tablespoons of butter in a saucepan and fry the vegetables and chopped giblet mixture (excluding the liver) gently for 5 minutes, until they start to brown. Add the red wine and water and keep at a rolling boil for about 30 minutes, skimming from time to time, until it is reduced by a quarter. Strain through a cheesecloth.

TO ROAST THE DUCK:
Roast the duck in the preheated oven at 500° for 40 minutes.

While the duck is cooking, remove the pits from all the olives and keep the pits. Blanch the green olives in boiling water for 5 minutes so they lose their bitterness. Put the Madeira and olive stones in a sauté pan and boil to reduce by half.

Add 1 cup of the duck stock and reduce again, then add the finely chopped liver to thicken the sauce. Season to taste with salt and pepper. Strain.

At the last minute, gradually add the remaining butter in small pieces, whisking vigorously all the time over a very low heat. Add all the olives.

Place the duck in a shallow serving dish and pour the sauce around it.

SERVES 4

ARTICHOKE HEARTS WITH YOUNG PEAS
Ragoût de fonds d'artichauts aux petits pois

To prepare the artichokes, first break off the stem close to the base. Starting from the bottom, remove the first few layers of hard leaves, then cut the artichoke across about halfway up, just above the heart. Using a small stainless steel knife, trim the artichoke all around, starting from the stem, to remove all the hard green parts and expose the paler heart. Do the same to the top of the artichoke until the choke is revealed. Remove the choke with the fingers or a spoon. Rub all the cut parts with lemon juice as you go along in order to prevent them from discoloring, then plunge the artichoke heart into water containing a dash of vinegar and let them soak while you prepare the rest.

Wash the mushrooms and slice them into fine pieces.

Drain the artichoke hearts and cut into quarters. Put them in a heavy-bottomed cast-iron saucepan with the olive oil. Season with salt and pepper, then cover and cook over a low heat for 15 minutes. Add the peas, cover again and continue cooking for 10 minutes. Add the mushrooms and cook for another 5 minutes, still over a low heat.

Serve in the saucepan after sprinkling with the chopped chervil.

SERVES 4

8 globe artichokes

1 lemon

Vinegar

$^1\!/_2$ cup button mushrooms

2 tablespoons olive oil

Salt

Freshly ground black pepper

1 cup tender young fresh green peas, shelled

Few sprigs of chervil, chopped

FILLET OF BEEF "BAUMANIÈRE"
Filet de boeuf "Baumanière"

1 carrot

1 shallot

1 onion

1 bottle good red Côtes du Rhone
   (or similar dry French wine)

2 chicken livers, chopped

6 anchovy fillets in olive oil, crushed

2 pounds fillet of beef

Olive oil

$\frac{1}{2}$ stick unsalted butter

Salt

Freshly ground black pepper

Preparation of the sauce should be started a day in advance to give the subtle flavors—especially the anchovies—time to develop and mature.

Peel the carrot, shallot, and onion and dice into small pieces. Put them in a saucepan with the red wine over a medium heat. Boil for 30 minutes to reduce, then thicken the sauce with the chicken livers. Add the crushed anchovy fillets and reduce for another few minutes, then sieve through a strainer. Refrigerate for 24 hours.

The following day, return the sauce to the heat and reduce it until it starts to really thicken (at this stage it should just cover the bottom of the pan). Be careful not to let it stick: stir it frequently with a wooden spatula.

Brush the meat with olive oil, then sauté it in more olive oil, cooking it well or lightly according to taste. Meanwhile, gradually add small pieces of softened butter to the sauce, whisking all the while with a sauce whisk.

Cut the meat into thick slices, season to taste with salt and pepper, pour the sauce over it and serve very hot.

SERVES 4 TO 6

LEG OF LAMB IN PUFF PASTRY
Gigot d'agneau en croûte

1 leg of very young lamb, $2\frac{1}{4}$ pounds
   or under

2 lamb kidneys

Unsalted butter

$\frac{1}{2}$ cup Madeira

Fresh or dried thyme

Fresh or dried rosemary

Salt

Freshly ground black pepper

Puff pastry

1 egg yolk

With a long, pointed knife, remove the bone from the leg of lamb. Cut the meat away from the bone until you reach the joint. Sever the joint and lift out the bone.

Preheat the oven to 500°, or its highest setting.

Dice the kidneys into fine pieces and fry them in a little butter for about 3 minutes. Deglaze the frying pan with the Madeira, adding thyme and rosemary to taste.

Fill the cavity left by the bone with this mixture. Sew the leg of lamb together again and season it with salt and pepper. Rub a little butter over it and put the lamb in the oven. Roast for about 15 minutes to seal the meat and draw out any water.

Roll out the puff pastry thinly to a size that is big enough to wrap up the lamb. Remove the lamb from the oven and wrap it in the puff pastry. Brush the top with the beaten egg. Return to the oven for 10 minutes to finish cooking.

SERVES 2

PIGEONS ROASTED WITH HONEY
Pigeons au miel

Grind the coriander and peppercorns in a pepper mill and stir them into the honey. Clean and truss the pigeons (or have the butcher do this).

Melt 4 tablespoons of the butter in a casserole dish. When it is foaming, add the pigeons and brown them on all sides. This should take about 5 or 6 minutes. When they are well browned, brush them with the honey, coriander, and pepper mixture. Cover, reduce the heat, and cook for about 30 minutes turning them from time to time. When they are cooked, remove the pigeons from the casserole and keep them warm.

Deglaze the casserole with the white wine. Add the stock and remaining butter. Put the pigeons back in the casserole and simmer for 2 more minutes.

SERVES 4

2 teaspoons whole coriander seeds

1 teaspoon black peppercorns

6 tablespoons honey

4 pigeons

5 tablespoons unsalted butter

$^1/_3$ cup dry white wine

1 tablespoon pigeon or chicken stock

ASPARAGUS CREAM SOUP WITH OYSTERS
Velouté d'asperges aux huîtres

Pare the asparagus stalks and wash in cold water. Cut off the tips and cook them in boiling salted water until tender. Drain, then plunge them into cold water. Drain well.

Dice the stalks and cook them gently in the butter in a large saucepan for about 3 minutes. Add the fish stock and let simmer for about 20 minutes. Add the crème fraîche and let simmer for 30 minutes or until the soup has a creamy consistency.

24 medium-sized asparagus spears

2 tablespoons unsalted butter

2 cups fish stock

2 cups crème fraîche

12 oysters

Salt

Freshly ground white pepper

Open the oysters and remove them from their shells. Warm them in their own juices for a few moments. Do not overcook them or they will become tough.

Sieve the asparagus soup through a strainer. Adjust the seasoning with salt and pepper, taking care not to add too much salt as the oysters are salty. Reheat the soup briefly.

Arrange 3 oysters and 6 asparagus tips in each soup plate and ladle the soup over. Serve hot.

SERVES 4

ALMOND TART WITH PINE NUTS
Tarte aux pignons

FOR THE PASTRY
²/₃ cup unsalted butter
1¹/₂ cups plain flour
2 tablespoons ground almonds
6 tablespoons superfine sugar
1 egg

Preheat the oven to 180°. Beat the butter until soft. Rub together the butter, flour, ground almonds, and 4 tablespoons of the sugar, working quickly and lightly.

Add the rest of the sugar and the egg, and mix together lightly, until the ingredients form a paste. Roll out the pastry with a rolling pin, preferably on a cool marble slab, and use it to line an 8- to 9-inch tart tin.

FOR THE ALMOND CREAM
7 tablespoons unsalted butter
7 tablespoons superfine sugar
7 tablespoons ground almonds
2 eggs
2 tablespoons rum
1¹/₂ tablespoons pine nuts

FOR THE ALMOND CREAM:
Cream the butter in a bowl until it is light and smooth. Beat in the sugar, then the ground almonds. Beat the mixture well until the ingredients are evenly distributed. Add one of the eggs and beat again for 3 to 4 minutes, until the mixture begins to increase in volume. Add the second egg and beat for another 3 to 4 minutes. Stir in the rum (or another spirit or liqueur if preferred, perhaps Grand Marnier or kirsch).

Spread the almond cream over the pastry and scatter the pine nuts over it, pushing them into the cream slightly so that they stay in place during cooking. Bake in a preheated oven for 30 to 40 minutes, until the tart is risen and brown. Cool before serving.

SERVES 4

Moulins de Mougins
Mougins

KIDNEYS AS COOKED AT THE MOULIN DE MOUGINS
Rognons de veau du Moulin

Remove all the fat and the skin from the kidneys, leaving them a shining rosy pink. Split each in two lengthways, starting from the edge where the fatty casing was attached. Remove as many of the little tubes, fibers, and fatty particles from the interior of the kidneys as you can without destroying their shape. Then, perpendicular to the first cut, slice them in $\frac{1}{4}$-inch-thick rounds—about the size of a French five-franc piece. Put the pieces on a plate and season with salt and pepper.

In a shallow pan with sloping sides, heat half the butter over high heat. When the foam subsides, put in half the seasoned kidneys. Let them sear thoroughly, then turn them with a wooden spatula. They should be cooked in 4 to 5 minutes. Drain the kidneys in a colander placed over a bowl to catch the juices and blood that will run out. Repeat the operation, using the remaining butter to cook the rest of the kidneys, and when they are cooked add them to the first batch in the colander. Keep hot.

Add the chopped shallots to the cooking juices in the pan, pour in the Calvados, and scrape up the butter and juices with the wooden spatula. Don't let the Calvados catch fire—that's not the object of the exercise. When the shallots have softened in the juices and the Calvados, add the cream and boil for 2 to 3 minutes, whisking all the time.

Strain the sauce through a fine sieve placed over a clean saucepan, working it through with the spatula. Add the Dijon mustard and whisk again to mix it in thoroughly. Add the kidneys to the sauce and heat through to just below boiling point. Taste for seasoning with salt and pepper. Add the chopped chervil, and serve on hot plates.

SERVES 2

2 veal kidneys (the flesh should be rosy and they should be robed generously in dry white fat)
2 tablespoons butter
2 tablespoons chopped shallots
3 generous tablespoons Calvados
5 tablespoons double cream
1 teaspoon Dijon mustard
Salt
Pepper
2 tablespoons coarsely chopped chervil

DUCK AS SERVED AT THE MOULIN DE MOUGINS

Le canard du Moulin

1 duck, 6 to 6½ pounds, plucked
    and cleaned

4 juniper berries

1 sprig thyme

Salt

Black pepper

3 tablespoons butter

1 cup full-bodied red wine

4 coarsely chopped shallots

1 teaspoon tomato purée

2 tablespoons cognac

1 chicken stock cube

Preheat the oven to 500°. Hold the duck in a gas jet to remove all the remaining stubs of feathers. Remove the feet, wing tips, and neck with a large knife. If the duck has not yet been gutted, do so, leaving in the heart, lungs, and liver. Place the juniper berries and thyme inside the duck and season it with salt and pepper, inside and out. Truss it with kitchen string.

Chop the wing tips and neck and put them in a roasting tin just large enough to hold the bird, and lay the duck on its side on top. Cover it with 1½ tablespoons of butter and place it in the hot oven. After 8 minutes, turn the duck over onto the other side, and after another 8 minutes place it breastside up and cook for another 10 minutes. This operation sears the duck all over and causes it to shed the excess fat in its skin.

Remove the duck and let it rest in a warm place for 10 minutes. Throw out the fat from the roasting tin and pour in the red wine, leaving in the wings and neck. Boil for a few minutes to deglaze the pan. Put to one side.

Remove the legs, cutting the skin carefully with a sharp knife, and set on one side. Remove the wishbone with the point of a small sharp knife. Skin the duck completely. Then carve five long slices from each breast, working parallel to the backbone. Keep hot.

Remove the heart, lungs, and liver, and set aside on a cutting board. Remove the juniper berries and the thyme and add them to the juices in the roasting tin.

Chop up the carcass with a heavy knife or cleaver. Heat the remaining butter in a saucepan and throw in the chopped carcass. Stir the pieces so they brown all over. Add the four coarsely chopped shallots and the tomato purée. Let the shallots brown a little, then flame with the cognac. When the flames have died down, add the wine from the roasting tin, together with the neck and the wing tips, and boil till you have no more than a coffee cup of liquid left. Add just enough hot water to cover the bones, and put in the stock cube. Boil for 20 minutes.

Meanwhile, chop the heart, lungs, and a quarter of the liver into fine pieces. When the 20 minutes are up, strain the contents of the roasting tin into another saucepan through a fine-wire sieve and then reduce again until no more than a coffee cup of the liquid remains. Add the chopped heart, lungs, and liver, bring to a boil again briefly and strain again, into a bowl. Season with a few turns of the peppermill—the sauce should already be salty enough—and keep the sauce hot in a bain-marie.

A quarter of an hour before you want to eat the dish, season the duck legs on the flesh side with coarse salt and grill for 15 minutes. During this time, divide the sauce between two hot plates and lay five slices of duck on each, making sure they are well bathed in the sauce. Place in a hot oven for a few minutes to heat through and serve. On a second plate, place the grilled duck legs, served simply with a green salad (curly endive or escarole) seasoned with wine vinegar and walnut oil.

SERVES 2

Pierre Orsi
Paris

RAVIOLI OF FOIE GRAS
Ravioles de foie gras

FOR THE SAUCE

Bring the port to a boil until it takes on a syrupy consistency. Add the veal stock and the bordelaise sauce. Stir. Add salt and pepper. Bring the sauce to a boil stirring continually until it emulsifies and coats the back of a spoon. Cut the truffles into julienne strips and add. Then add the ³/₄ cup of the combined diced goose-and-duck foie gras. Stir and keep warm.

FOR THE BORDELAISE SAUCE

Heat 4 tablespoons of the butter in a saucepan and cook the shallots until softened. Add the wine, thyme, and peppercorns. Bring to a boil and reduce by half. Add the stock, and simmer gently for about 30 minutes. Remove the thyme sprigs. Add the remaining 3 tablespoons of butter, and salt and pepper, and whisk well.

FOR THE RAVIOLI

Roll out the ravioli sheets on a surface lightly dusted with flour. Cut 12 circles, approximately 4 inches across, with a sharp cutter. Brush each one with the whipped egg yolks. Dice the remaining duck and goose foie gras and spread

FOR THE SAUCE

1¹/₂ cups port

1¹/₂ cups veal stock (made from veal bones and vegetables), reduced until slightly syrupy

1 cup bordelaise sauce (see recipe below)

Salt

Freshly ground pepper

³/₄ cup black truffles

³/₄ cup of the duck and goose foie gras, combined, from the ingredients listed below

FOR THE BORDELAISE SAUCE

7 tablespoons butter

3 tablespoons shallots, finely chopped

1¹/₄ cups good red Bordeaux wine

2 sprigs of thyme

3 black peppercorns, crushed

1¹/₄ cups veal or beef stock

Salt

Pepper

FOR THE RAVIOLI

12 sheets of ravioli dough

2 egg yolks, whipped

12 ounces or 1 1/2 cups of duck foie gras

8 ounces or 1 cup of goose foie gras

4 tablespoons melted unsalted butter

2 chicken-stock cubes

about 2 soup spoons each on 6 of the circles. Place a second circle over each of the filled ravioli, and pinch all around the edges to seal. Brush the ravioli with the melted butter to keep the dough moist. Keep in a cool place.

Bring to a boil 5 pints of water in which you have dissolved the chicken cubes or the stock powder. Drop the ravioli gently into the boiling stock. Cook for 3 to 4 minutes. Lift each one with a slotted spoon into a soup plate, and ladle the warm sauce over the ravioli.

SERVES 6

SEA BASS WITH VIRGIN OLIVE OIL
Loup de mer à l'huile d'olive vierge

3 leeks, the white part only

4 fillets of sea bass, about 6 ounces each

2 tablespoons butter

Salt

Freshly ground pepper

1/2 cup of extra virgin olive oil

3 ounces caviar

Cut the leeks into julienne strips and wash. Skin the sea bass fillets. Put the butter in a casserole with 4 soup spoons of water, and salt and pepper, and bring to a boil. Add the leeks and simmer gently for 2 to 3 minutes.

Place the oil in a pan and heat. Salt and pepper the fish, and place in the pan to cook for 3 to 4 minutes. When cooked, remove to a hot dish. Drain the leeks well, and place around the fish. Garnish the fish with caviar.

SERVES 4

SAVARIN WITH FIG COMPOTE

Savarins à la compote tiède de figues

Put all the ingredients for the savarin together in a mixer.

Separate the dough into individual balls about the size of an espresso cup and flatten slightly, making a small indentation in the center. Place in a hot oven for 10 to 15 minutes.

To make the syrup, boil the water with the sugar and the vanilla pod until it reaches a syrupy consistency. Spoon the syrup over the cooked savarins. Fill the cavity with crème fraîche, and a spoonful of fig compote. Serve with a ball of vanilla ice cream.

SERVES 4 TO 6

SAVARIN

1 cup flour

5 tablespoons butter

3 eggs

1 teaspoon salt

1 teaspoon sugar

1 teaspoon yeast

½ cup warm milk

SYRUP

3¾ cups water

¼ cup sugar

1 vanilla pod

Crème fraîche

Fig compote

Vanilla ice cream

Apicius
Paris

SPICE-CRUSTED COD

Morue en croûte d'épices

If using a bamboo steamer for this recipe, be sure to soak it in water beforehand to avoid scorching the wood.

In a bowl toss fillets with sea salt to coat. Let fillets stand, covered, 30 minutes.

FOR THE SPICE RUB:

In a small bowl stir together spice-rub ingredients.

FOR THE DRESSING:

In a small bowl whisk together lemon juice and soy sauce until combined and gradually whisk in oil. Season dressing with salt and pepper.

6 skinless 6-ounce center-cut cod fillets

½ pound coarse sea salt

FOR THE SPICE RUB

½ teaspoon celery salt

½ teaspoon cinnamon

¼ teaspoon curry powder

⅛ teaspoon table salt

⅛ teaspoon freshly ground black pepper

FOR THE DRESSING

1/4 cup fresh lemon juice

2 tablespoons soy sauce

1/4 cup pure peanut oil

1 scallion

20 small fresh basil leaves

20 small fresh mint leaves

20 fresh flat-leafed parsley leaves

20 fresh cilantro leaves

1/2 pound baby spinach
(about 8 cups packed)

Diagonally slice scallion and in a small bowl toss with herbs. Rinse cod under cold water and pat dry. Sprinkle spice rub evenly over cod and arrange in one layer in a large steamer lined with parchment paper. Steam cod over simmering water until just cooked through, 8 to 10 minutes.

While cod is steaming, in a large bowl toss spinach with dressing and salt and pepper to taste. Mound spinach on 6 large plates and top with cod and herb mixture.

SERVES 6

PÂTE DE POMME À LA JEANNE MOREAU

1/2 cup butter

2 rolls of ready-made flaky pastry

12 white new potatoes, medium size,
    and 2 more for good luck

1 pound of heavy thick cream (it sticks
    to the spoon and is very rich)

Salt

Ground black pepper

1 teacup of chopped, fresh chervil

2 egg yolks

Milk

Crème fraîche

Take a pie plate with a removable bottom and butter it generously with softened butter. Lay the first layer of pastry on the bottom of the buttered pie plate. Peel the potatoes and slice them—not too thick, not too thin. Dry them in a large kitchen towel.

Spread 3 or 4 tablespoons of heavy thick cream onto the bottom layer of pastry shell. Salt, pepper, and sprinkle with chopped chervil. Then add one layer of potatoes, then more cream, salt, pepper, and chervil. Continue this until you have finished with the potatoes. Then cover with a top layer of pastry shell that you have snipped with the design of your choice (or the design below. See attached drawing showing appropriate way to snip pastry shell). This allows for the evaporation of steam during cooking.

Before placing in the oven, brush the top with a mixture of egg yolks and milk to give it a golden brown color during cooking. Cook for 60 minutes (at least) in an oven set at 350°. To verify that it is done, check with a sharp knife.

Serve hot with a bowl of crème fraîche so that each person can take as much as desired.

This pâte should be served with a green salad with walnut oil. Serve with a wine from Touraine—chilled and red!

1. Fold pastry sheet in half twice

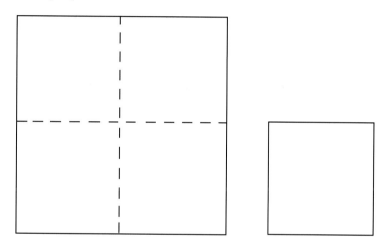

2. Make the following snips

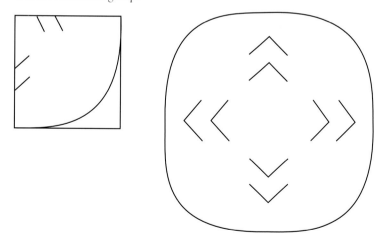

3. When unfolded, the pastry should look like this